LAST ESSAYS

I wonder who ~~say they now~~ to talk.
~~that~~ have been in ironmonger
with a ~~to~~ a new opening for
his trade

He must have been an ironmonger
trying for what ~~onset~~ for his wares.
And to ~~what~~ ~~audience~~. Personally
I would have been afraid to tell
it to ~~whitehorse~~ — Meaning that ~~themselves~~
which is ~~themselves~~ for ~~it~~ ~~capable~~ to
swallow anything in the way of a
yarn.

LAST ESSAYS

BY
JOSEPH CONRAD

WITH AN INTRODUCTION
BY
RICHARD CURLE

40629

GARDEN CITY   NEW YORK
DOUBLEDAY, PAGE & COMPANY
1926

CONTENTS

40629

INTRODUCTION

MOST of the contents of this volume were written subsequent to the publication of "Notes on Life and Letters" in 1921, and these two books together may be said to contain practically all Conrad's miscellaneous writings. There are, it is true, a few short prefaces and some interesting letters to newspapers which might have been included here, but they are of no particular importance, and the twenty separate pieces gathered between these covers are indeed the last essays of Joseph Conrad. But there remains a chance that some of his early essays and reviews may still rest undiscovered in the files of old newspapers and weeklies. Conrad had a very uncertain memory for his own work, and I recall that when the material for "Notes on Life and Letters" was being collected, he was frequently quite vague as to what he had written and where it had appeared. In proof of this, it may be mentioned that the essay entitled "John Galsworthy" in this volume was omitted from the previous one only through Conrad's forgetfulness of its existence. Therefore, as I say, discoveries may yet be made.

In the latter years of his life Conrad occasionally found relief from the toil and exhaustion of more creative work in the writing of reminiscent essays, and some of these rank, decidedly, among his finest efforts in this direction. "Last Essays" is just as remarkable a book as "Notes on Life and Letters"; it contains passages of extraordinary charm, serenity, and eloquence. And particular care has been taken to avoid any aspect of absolute completeness, as though a dead author's desk had been ransacked for every fragment: all the articles included in this volume have been included for very definite reasons. Nothing has been printed merely for the purpose of adding to the bulk.

For some time Conrad had had the idea of writing a pendent volume to "The Mirror of the Sea," and the unfinished article, "Legends," on which he was at work the day before he died, was, he told me, to have formed part of such a book. And I suspect that "The *Torrens*," "Christmas Day at Sea," "Ocean Travel," "Outside Literature," and part, at least, of "Geography and Some Explorers," would also have been incorporated in this book, and therefore I have placed them all together at the beginning of the volume. They form, as it were, the shadowy nucleus of a projected work.

"Geography and Some Explorers," the second longest essay in this collection, was written as a general introduction to a serial work called "Countries of the World." It appeared as "The Romance of Travel" in the first number, February, 1924, and was reprinted under its proper title in *The National Geographic Magazine*, March, 1924. In this fascinating essay, Conrad, after discussing the feats of some of the early navigators and explorers, gives a memorable account of a passage he made in 1888 (when in command of the *Otago*) through the Torres Straits on a voyage from Sydney to Mauritius.

"The *Torrens*: A Personal Tribute," was published in *The Blue Peter*, October, 1923. In the early 'nineties Conrad had been chief officer of this ship—he joined her on November 2, 1891, and left her on October 15, 1893— and he made two journeys from England to Australia and back in that capacity. For her he always retained a warm affection, and when, in the September *Blue Peter* of 1923, there was issued a coloured illustration of the *Torrens*, he willingly consented to give a personal remembrance of her in the next number. The last words, in which he describes her end upon the shores of the Mediterranean, possess a rare and pensive beauty, which I recover in the following paragraph:

"But in the end her body of iron and wood, so fair to look upon, had to be broken up—I hope with fitting reverence; and as I sit here, thirty years, almost to a day, since I last set eyes on her, I love to think that her perfect form found a merciful end on the shores of the Sunlit Sea of my boyhood's dreams, and that her fine spirit has returned to dwell in the regions of the great winds, the inspirers and companions of her swift, re-nowned, sea-tossed life which I, too, have been per-mitted to share for a little while."

"Christmas Day at Sea" was published in the London *Daily Mail* on December 24, 1923. It was concerned largely with an episode on one Christmas Day during Conrad's first voyage to Australia in the *Duke of Suth-erland* in 1879, where he served as an A. B.

"Ocean Travel" made its first appearance in the London *Evening News* of May 15, 1923, where it was named "My Hotel in Mid-Atlantic." It was written during Conrad's voyage to America in the *Tuscania* in the spring of that year, and was posted to me the mo-ment he arrived in New York. It compares the old and the new life at sea, and, needless to say, the vote of affection is given for the old.

"Outside Literature," a short essay dealing with the subject of notices to mariners, appeared under the title "Notices to Mariners" in the *Manchester Guardian* of December 4, 1922, and under its proper title in the American *Bookman* of February, 1923.

"Legends," as I have mentioned, was the last article Conrad ever wrote; it was left unfinished upon his desk. It tells, with a strain of melancholy, of the breed of seamen who have disappeared with the disappearance of sailing ships, and was printed, less than a fortnight after Conrad's death, in the London *Daily Mail* of August 15, 1924.

Next follow two essays which have the war at sea as background. "The Unlighted Coast" recalls Conrad's experiences in the North Sea during his ten-days' cruise in the *Ready* in 1917—a full account of this cruise is to be found in Captain Sutherland's "At Sea with Joseph Conrad"—and was written for the Admiralty. For some reason or other they never used it and it first saw the light in the London *Times* of August 18, 1925.

"The Dover Patrol," written at the request of the late Lord Northcliffe, was published in the London *Times* of July 27, 1921, the day on which the Prince of Wales unveiled the Dover Patrol Memorial. It is a glowing tribute to "the physical endurance, the inborn seamanship, the matter-of-fact, industrious, indefatigable enthusiasm" of the men who guarded unsleepingly and at extreme hazard the entrance to the Channel.

The "Memorandum on the Scheme for Fitting Out a Sailing Ship" is here first printed. Written in 1919 for the Holt Steamship Company, who had proposed to fit out a sailing ship for the training of boys destined for the Mercantile Marine, it is an example of Conrad's intense and practical interest in such subjects. It is exactly what it purports to be—a memorandum, precise, technical, full of his accumulated experience and long-pondered ideas. Nothing came of the scheme: as Mr. Lawrence Holt wrote to me, it was "abandoned owing to the depression of trade which set in soon after my conversation with Mr. Conrad." The document

from then to now has been in Mr. Holt's possession, and
cordial thanks are due to him for his permission to use
it here.

"The Loss of the *Dalgonar*" is a further example of
Conrad's interest in questions of seamanship. Indeed,
I print it solely for that reason, because, in itself, it but
refers to the contents of an article from another pen. It
appeared, as a letter to the editor, in the London
Mercury of December, 1921, and was called forth by a
paper in the September issue entitled "A True Story:
Log and Record of the Wreck of the Ship *Dalgonar* of
Liverpool, bound from Callao to Taltal." This paper
described the wreck of the barque *Loire*, which happened in October, 1913; and Conrad's letter, while
correcting some obvious mistakes in the narrative as
printed, is a testimony to the gallantry and efficiency of
the officers and crew.

The essay called "Travel" was written, I am proud
to think, out of friendship for myself, and formed the
preface to a book by me, "Into the East: Notes on
Burma and Malaya," 1923. The effort to finish "The
Rover" held up the writing of this preface for about a
year, but it seems to me that in its evocation of the
great travellers of old and of times that have gone for
ever it reaches the highest beauty and distinction. Let
me quote one paragraph:

"And those things, which stand as if imperishable
in the pages of old books of travel, are all blown away;
have vanished as utterly as the smoke of the travellers'
camp fires in the icy night air of the Gobi Desert, as the
smell of incense burned in the temples of strange gods,
as the voices of Asiatic statesmen speculating with the
cruel wisdom of past ages on matters of peace and war."

"Stephen Crane," the longest and most elaborate
essay in the book, was written as an introduction to

Mr. Thomas Beer's "Stephen Crane, a Study in American Letters," 1923. Conrad, as is generally known, was a close friend of Crane during the last years of that meteoric life, when Crane was frequently a neighbour of his in southern England. In all, he wrote three essays on Crane and his work. One appeared in "Notes on Life and Letters," two are printed in this volume, and all breathe a spirit of affectionate admiration. This essay is a study in biographical sidelights and is undoubtedly the most personal and the most delightful of all reminiscences of Crane.

The short essay, "His War Book," which follows, was composed specifically as a preface to a new edition of Crane's best-known work, "The Red Badge of Courage"—the new edition came out at last in 1925—and it gives clear indication of Conrad's feeling for the artist who could observe so truly and create with such economy.

"John Galsworthy," as I have said, was only accidentally omitted from the previous volume of Conrad's essays. It was composed as a review of "A Man of Property," contained in a wider study of the author, and was published in the London *Outlook* of March 31, 1906, under the title of "A Middle Class Family." A few years before he died, Conrad rectified, as far as he could, his oversight by privately printing about fifty copies of this essay, and he would certainly have included it in any future volume of essays.

The next piece, "A Glance at Two Books," dealing with Galsworthy's "The Island Pharisees" and Hudson's "Green Mansions," dates from even earlier and was done in 1904. Written obviously in answer to an editorial request, it was, for reasons unknown, never used, and the typescript, being found among Conrad's papers, was first printed in *T. P.'s and Cassell's Weekly* of August 1, 1925.

A "Preface to his Shorter Tales" was written at the instigation of his American publishers to introduce "The Shorter Tales of Joseph Conrad," and the essay, like the selection, has never appeared in England. It was one of his last completed pieces—the volume was issued after his death in 1924—and it throws a reminiscent glance upon the ideas that animated his work and upon his writing life.

The little note, "Cookery," charming in its playful fancy, was a send-off to his wife's book, "A Handbook of Cookery for a Small House," 1922. I include it here for the sake of its association and for the unique quality of its tone.

The next two pieces, both of them letters, give glimpses of Conrad's abiding interest in international questions and the affairs of Europe. He was always a student of foreign politics, a student fortified by an impressive historical sense and by a great knowledge of continental problems throughout the centuries, and these two letters, with their combined eloquence and hold upon reality, throw light upon an aspect of Conrad's mind of which few people are aware.

The first letter, an appeal for a free Constantinople under the protection of the Powers, was published in the London *Times* of November 7, 1912, when the Balkan States were at war with Turkey and their armies already within striking distance of her capital.

The second letter, written evidently a few days later to an untraceable correspondent—a typescript only was found—who had criticized his printed observations, is an amplification of the previous letter.

Finally comes "The Congo Diary," a reprint of the diary kept by Conrad in the Congo in 1890, which was first published in *The Blue Peter*, October, 1925, and then in *The Yale Review*, January, 1926. This diary calls for its own introduction and a series of explanatory notes, and these will be found with it at the end of the book.

Here, then, are the twenty pieces which compose this volume of "Last Essays." They show as clearly as did the contents of "Notes on Life and Letters" the rich diversity of Conrad's mind, his powers of cogent argument, of fond memory, and of noble expression. His mastery over his chosen material never flagged and these essays are a last witness to his consummate gifts.

RICHARD CURLE.

LAST ESSAYS

LAST ESSAYS

GEOGRAPHY AND SOME EXPLORERS

It is safe to say that for the majority of mankind the superiority of geography over geometry lies in the appeal of its figures. It may be an effect of the incorrigible frivolity inherent in human nature, but most of us will agree that a map is more fascinating to look at than a figure in a treatise on conic sections—at any rate for the simple minds which are all the equipment of the majority of the dwellers on this earth.

No doubt a trigonometrical survey may be a romantic undertaking, striding over deserts and leaping over valleys never before trodden by the foot of civilized man; but its accurate operations can never have for us the fascination of the first hazardous steps of a venturesome, often lonely, explorer jotting down by the light of his camp fire the thoughts, the impressions, and the toil of his day.

For a long time yet a few suggestive words grappling with things seen will have the advantage over a long array of precise, no doubt interesting, and even profitable figures. The earth is a stage, and though it may be an advantage, even to the right comprehension of the play, to know its exact configuration, it is the drama of human endeavour that will be the thing, with a ruling passion expressed by outward action marching perhaps blindly to success or failure, which themselves are often undistinguishable from each other at first.

1

Of all the sciences, geography finds its origin in action, and what is more, in adventurous action of the kind that appeals to sedentary people who like to dream of arduous adventure in the manner of prisoners dreaming behind bars of all the hardships and hazards of liberty dear to the heart of man.

Descriptive geography, like any other kind of science, has been built on the experience of certain phenomena and on experiments prompted by that unappeasable curiosity of men which their intelligence has elevated into a quite respectable passion for acquiring knowledge. Like other sciences it has fought its way to truth through a long series of errors. It has suffered from the love of the marvellous, from our credulity, from rash and unwarrantable assumptions, from the play of unbridled fancy.

Geography had its phase of circumstantially extravagant speculation which had nothing to do with the pursuit of truth, but has given us a curious glimpse of the mediæval mind playing in its ponderous childish way with the problems of our earth's shape, its size, its character, its products, its inhabitants. Cartography was almost as pictorial then as are some modern newspapers. It crowded its maps with pictures of strange pageants, strange trees, strange beasts, drawn with amazing precision in the midst of theoretically conceived continents. It delineated imaginary kingdoms of Monomotapa and of Prester John, the regions infested by lions or haunted by unicorns, inhabited by men with reversed feet, or eyes in the middle of their breasts.

All this might have been amusing if the mediæval gravity in the absurd had not been in itself a wearisome thing. But what of that! Has not the key science of modern chemistry passed through its dishonest phase of Alchemy (a portentous development of the confidence trick), and our knowledge of the starry sky been arrived at through the superstitious idealism of Astrology looking for men's fate in the depths of the infinite? Mere megalomania on a colossal scale. Yet, solemn fooling for solemn fooling of the scientific order, I prefer the kind that does not lay itself out to thrive on the fears and the cupidities of men.

From that point of view geography is the most blameless of sciences. Its fabulous phase never aimed at cheating simple mortals (who are a multitude) out of their peace of mind or their money. At the most it has enticed some of them away from their homes; to death may be, now and then to a little disputed glory, not seldom to contumely, never to high fortune. The greatest of them all, who has presented modern geography with a new world to work upon, was at one time loaded with chains and thrown into prison. Columbus remains a pathetic figure, not a sufferer in the cause of geography, but a victim of the imperfections of jealous human hearts, accepting his fate with resignation. Among explorers he appears lofty in his troubles and like a man of a kingly nature. His contribution to the knowledge of the earth was certainly royal. And if the discovery of America was the occasion of the greatest outburst of reckless cruelty and greed known to history we may say this at least for it, that the gold of Mexico and Peru, unlike the gold of alchemists, was really there, palpable, yet, as ever, the most elusive of the Fata Morgana that lure men away from their homes, as a moment of reflection will convince any one. For nothing is more certain than that there will never be enough gold to go round, as the Conquistadores found out by experience.

I suppose it is not very charitable of me, but I must

say that to this day I feel a malicious pleasure at the many disappointments of those pertinacious searchers for El Dorado who climbed mountains, pushed through forests, swam rivers, floundered in bogs, without giving a single thought to the science of geography. Not for them the serene joys of scientific research, but infinite toil, in hunger, thirst, sickness, battle; with broken heads, unseemly squabbles, and empty pockets in the end. I cannot help thinking it served them right. It is an ugly tale, which has not much to do with the service of geography. The geographical knowledge of our day is of the kind that would have been beyond the conception of the hardy followers of Cortés and Pizarro; and of that most estimable of Conquerors who was called Cabeza de Vaca, who was high-minded and dealt humanely with the heathen nations whose territories he traversed in search of one more El Dorado. It is said they loved him greatly, but now the very memory of those nations is gone from the earth, while their territories, which they could not take with them, are being traversed many times every twenty-four hours by the trains of the Southern Pacific railroad.

The discovery of the New World marks the end of the fabulous geography, and it must be owned that the history of the Conquest contains at least one great moment—I mean a geographically great moment— when Vasco Núñez de Balboa, while crossing the Isthmus of Panama, set his eyes for the first time upon the ocean, the immensity of which he did not suspect, and which in his elation he named the Pacific. It is anything but that; but the privileged Conquistador cannot be blamed for surrendering to his first impression.

The Gulf of Panama, which is what he really saw with that first glance, is one of the calmest spots on the waters of the globe. Too calm. The old navigators dreaded it as a dangerous region where one might be caught and lie becalmed for weeks with one's crew dying slowly of thirst under a cloudless sky. The worst of fates, this, to feel yourself die in a long and helpless agony. How much preferable a region of storms where man and ship can at least put up a fight and remain defiant almost to the last.

I must not be understood to mean that a tempest at sea is a delightful experience, but I would rather face the fiercest tempest than a gulf pacific even to deadliness, a prison-house for incautious caravels and a place of torture for their crews. But Balboa was charmed with its serene aspect. He did not know where he was. He probably thought himself within a stone's throw, as it were, of the Indies and Cathay. Or did he perhaps, like a man touched with grace, have a moment of exalted vision, the awed feeling that what he was looking at was an abyss of waters comparable in its extent to the view of the unfathomable firmament, and sown all over with groups of islands resembling the constellations of the sky?

But whatever spiritual glimpse of the truth he might have had, Balboa could not possibly know that this great moment of his life had added suddenly thousands of miles to the circumference of the globe, had opened an immense theatre for the human drama of adventure and exploration, a field for the missionary labours of, mainly, Protestant churches, and spread an enormous canvas on which armchair geographers could paint the most fanciful variants of their pet theory of a great southern continent.

I will not quarrel with the post-Columbian cartographers for their wild but, upon the whole, interesting inventions. The provocation to let one's self go was

considerable. Geography militant, which had succeeded the geography fabulous, did not seem able
to accept the idea that there was much more water
than land on this globe. Nothing could satisfy their
sense of the fitness of things but an enormous extent
of solid earth which they placed in that region of the
South where, as a matter of fact, the great white-crested
seas of stormy latitudes will be free to chase each other
all round the globe to the end of time. I suppose
their landsmen's temperament stood in the way of their
recognition that the world of geography, so far as the
apportioning of space goes, seems to have been planned
mostly for the convenience of fishes.

What is surprising to me is that the seamen of the
time should have really believed that the large continents to the north of the Equator demanded, as a
matter of good art or else of sound science, to be
balanced by corresponding masses of land in the
southern hemisphere. They were simple souls. The
chorus of armchair people all singing the same tune
made them blind to the many plain signs of a great open
sea. Every bit of coast-line discovered, every mountain-
top glimpsed in the distance, had to be dragged loyally
into the scheme of the Terra Australis Incognita.

Even Tasman, the best seaman of them all before
James Cook, the most accomplished of seventeenth-
century explorers and navigators that went forth to
settle the geography of the Pacific—even Tasman,
after coming unexpectedly upon the North Island of
New Zealand, and lingering long enough there to
chart roughly a bit of the coast and lose a boat's crew
in a sudden affray with the Maoris, seemed to take it
for granted that this was the western limit of an
enormous continent extending away towards the point
of South America.

Mighty is the power of a theory, especially if based on such a common-sense notion as the balance of continents. And it must be remembered that it is difficult for us now to realize not only the navigational dangers of unknown seas, but the awful geographical incertitudes of the first explorers in that new world of waters.

Tasman's journal, which was published not so very long ago, gives us some idea of their perplexing difficulties. The early navigators had no means of ascertaining their exact position on the globe. They could calculate their latitude, but the problem of longitude was a matter which bewildered their minds and often falsified their judgment. It had to be a matter of pure guesswork. Tasman and his officers, when they met on board the *Heemskirk*, anchored in Murderers' Bay, to consider their further course in the light of their instructions, did not know where any of the problematic places named in their instructions were, neither did they know where they themselves were.

Tasman might have sailed north or east, but in the end he decided to sail between the two, and, circling about, returned to Batavia, where he was received coldly by his employers, the honourable governor-general and the council in Batavia. Their final judgment was that Abel Tasman was a skilful navigator, but that he had shown himself "remiss" in his investigations, and that he had been guilty of leaving certain problems unsolved.

We are told that Tasman did not expect this armchair criticism; and indeed, even now, it seems surprising to an unprejudiced mind. It was the voyage during which, among other things, Tasman discovered the island by which his name lives on the charts, took first contact with New Zealand (which was not seen again till 130 years afterwards), sailed over many thousands of miles of uncharted seas, bringing back with him a journal which was of much value afterwards for his exploring successors.

It may be he was hurt by the verdict of the honourable council, but he does not seem to have been cast down by it, for it appears that shortly afterwards he asked for a rise of salary—and, what is still more significant, he got it. He was obviously a valuable servant, but I am sorry to say that his character as a man was not of the kind to cause governors and councils to treat him with particular consideration. Except in professional achievement he is not comparable to Captain Cook, a humble son of the soil like himself, but a modest man of genius, the familiar associate of the most learned in the land, medallist of the Royal Society, and a captain in the Royal Navy.

But there was a taint of an unscrupulous adventurer in Tasman. It is certain that at various times his patron, the Governor Anthony van Diemen, and the honourable council in Batavia, had employed him in some shady transactions of their own, connected with the Japan trade. There is also no doubt that once he had, on his own responsibility, kidnapped an influential Chinaman who stood in the way of some business negotiation Tasman was conducting with the Sultan of Achin.

The Chinaman may have been a worthless person, but one wonders what happened to him in the end; and, in any case, the proceeding is open to criticism. Then in his old age he got into some disreputable scrape which caused the congregation with which he worshipped to ask him to resign his membership. Even the honourable council was startled, and dismissed him from his employment, though characteristically enough not actually from their service. This action of the council fixes the character of the man better than any scandalous story. He was valuable, but compromising.

All these regrettable details came to my knowledge quite recently in a very amusing and interesting book, but I must confess that my early admiration for Tasman as one of the early fathers of militant geography has not been affected very much by it. Remiss or not, he had in the course of his voyages mapped 8,000 miles of an island which by common consent is called now a continent, a geologically very old continent indeed, but which is now the home of a very young commonwealth with all the possibilities of material and intellectual splendour still hidden in its future.

I like to think that in that portion of the Elysian Fields set apart for great navigators, James Cook would not refuse to acknowledge the civilities of Abel Tasman, a fellow seaman who had first reported the existence of New Zealand in the perplexed, bewildered way of those times, 130 years before Captain Cook on his second voyage laid for ever the ghost of the Terra Australis Incognita and added New Zealand to the scientific domain of the geography triumphant of our day.

No shade of remissness nor doubtful motive rests upon the achievements of Captain Cook, who came out of a labourer's cottage to take his place at the head of the masters of maritime exploration who worked at the great geographical problem of the Pacific. *Endeavour* was the name of the ship which carried him on his first voyage, and it was also the watchword of his professional life. *Resolution* was the name of the ship he commanded himself on his second expedition, and it was the determining quality of his soul. I will not say that it was the greatest, because he had all the other manly qualities of a great man.

The voyages of the early explorers were prompted by an acquisitive spirit, the idea of lucre in some form, the desire of trade or the desire of loot, disguised in more or less fine words. But Cook's three voyages are free from any taint of that sort. His aims needed no disguise. They were scientific. His deeds speak for themselves with the masterly simplicity of a hard-won success. In that respect he seems to belong to the single-minded explorers of the nineteenth century, the late fathers of militant geography whose only object was the search for truth. Geography is a science of facts, and they devoted themselves to the discovery of facts in the configuration and features of the main continents.

It was the century of landsmen investigators. In saying this I do not forget the polar explorers, whose aims were certainly as pure as the air of those high latitudes where not a few of them laid down their lives for the advancement of geography. Seamen, men of science, it is difficult to speak of them without admirative emotion. The dominating figure among the seamen explorers of the first half of the nineteenth century is that of another good man, Sir John Franklin, whose fame rests not only on the extent of his discoveries, but on professional prestige and high personal character. This great navigator, who never returned home, served geography even in his death. The persistent efforts extending over ten years to ascertain his fate advanced greatly our knowledge of the polar regions.

As gradually revealed to the world this fate appeared the more tragic in this, that for the first two years the

way of the *Erebus* and *Terror* expedition seemed to be
the way to the desired and important success, while in
truth it was all the time the way of death, the end of
the darkest drama perhaps played behind the curtain of
Arctic mystery.

The last words unveiling the mystery of the *Erebus*
and *Terror* expedition were brought home and disclosed
to the world by Sir Leopold McClintock, in his book,
"The Voyage of the *Fox* in the Arctic Seas." It is a
little book, but it records with manly simplicity the
tragic ending of a great tale. It so happened that I
was born in the year of its publication. Therefore, I
may be excused for not getting hold of it till ten years
afterwards. I can only account for it falling into my
hands by the fact that the fate of Sir John Franklin was
a matter of European interest, and that Sir Leopold
McClintock's book was translated, I believe, into every
language of the white races.

My copy was probably in French. But I have read
the work many times since. I have now on my shelves
a copy of a popular edition got up exactly as I remember
my first one. It contains the touching facsimile of the
printed form filled in with a summary record of the two
ships' work, the name of "Sir John Franklin commanding the expedition" written in ink, and the pathetic
underlined entry "All well." It was found by Sir
Leopold McClintock under a cairn and it is dated just a
year before the two ships had to be abandoned in their
deadly ice-trap, and their crews' long and desperate
struggle for life began.

There could hardly have been imagined a better book
for letting in the breath of the stern romance of polar
exploration into the existence of a boy whose knowledge
of the poles of the earth had been till then of an abstract
formal kind as mere imaginary ends of the imaginary

axis upon which the earth turns. The great spirit of the realities of the story sent me off on the romantic explorations of my inner self; to the discovery of the taste of poring over maps; and revealed to me the existence of a latent devotion to geography which interfered with my devotion (such as it was) to my other schoolwork.

Unfortunately, the marks awarded for that subject were almost as few as the hours apportioned to it in the school curriculum by persons of no romantic sense for the real, ignorant of the great possibilities of active life; with no desire for struggle, no notion of the wide spaces of the world—mere bored professors, in fact, who were not only middle-aged but looked to me as if they had never been young. And their geography was very much like themselves, a bloodless thing with a dry skin covering a repulsive armature of uninteresting bones.

I would be ashamed of my warmth in digging up a hatchet which has been buried now for nearly fifty years if those fellows had not tried so often to take my scalp at the yearly examinations. There are things that one does not forget. And besides, the geography which I had discovered for myself was the geography of open spaces and wide horizons built up on men's devoted work in the open air, the geography still militant but already conscious of its approaching end with the death of the last great explorer. The antagonism was radical.

Thus it happened that I got no marks at all for my first and only paper on Arctic geography, which I wrote at the age of thirteen. I still think that for my tender years it was an erudite performance. I certainly did know something of Arctic geography, but what I was after really, I suppose, was the history of Arctic exploration. My knowledge had considerable gaps, but I managed to compress my enthusiasm into just two pages, which in itself was a sort of merit. Yet I got no marks. For one thing it was not a set subject. I believe the only comment made about it to my private tutor was that I seemed to have been wasting my time in reading books of travel instead of attending to my studies. I tell you, those fellows were always trying to take my scalp. On another occasion I just saved it by proficiency in map-drawing. It must have been good, I suppose; but all I remember about it is that it was done in a loving spirit.

I have no doubt that star-gazing is a fine occupation, for it leads you within the borders of the unattainable. But map-gazing, to which I became addicted so early, brings the problems of the great spaces of the earth into stimulating and directing contact with sane curiosity and gives an honest precision to one's imaginative faculty. And the honest maps of the nineteenth century nourished in me a passionate interest in the truth of geographical facts and a desire for precise knowledge which was extended later to other subjects.

For a change had come over the spirit of cartographers. From the middle of the eighteenth century on the business of map-making had been growing into an honest occupation, registering the hard-won knowledge, but also in a scientific spirit recording the geographical ignorance of its time. And it was Africa, the continent out of which the Romans used to say some new thing was always coming, that got cleared of the dull imaginary wonders of the dark ages, which were replaced by exciting spaces of white paper. Regions unknown! My imagination could depict to itself there worthy, adventurous and devoted men, nibbling at the edges, attacking from north and south and east and west, conquering a bit of truth here and a bit of truth there, and sometimes swallowed up by the mystery their hearts were so persistently set on unveiling.

Among them Mungo Park, of western Sudan, and Bruce, of Abyssinia, were, I believe, the first friends I made when I began to take notice—I mean geographical notice—of the continents of the world into which I was born. The fame of these two had already been for a long time European, and their figures had become historical by then. But their story was a very novel thing to me, for the very latest geographical news that could have been whispered to me in my cradle was that of the expedition of Burton and Speke, the news of the existence of Tanganyika and of Victoria Nyanza.

I stand here confessed as a contemporary of the Great Lakes. Yes, I could have heard of their discovery in my cradle, and it was only right that, grown to a boy's estate, I should have in the later sixties done my first bit of map-drawing and paid my first homage to the prestige of their first explorers. It consisted in entering laboriously in pencil the outline of Tanganyika on my beloved old atlas, which, having been published in 1852, knew nothing, of course, of the Great Lakes. The heart of its Africa was white and big.

Surely it could have been nothing but a romantic impulse which prompted the idea of bringing it up to date with all the accuracy of which I was capable. Thus I could imagine myself stepping in the very footprints of geographical discovery. And it was not all wasted time. As a bit of prophetic practice it was not bad for me. Many years afterwards, as second officer in the Merchant Service, it was my duty to correct and bring up to date the charts of more than one ship, according to the Admiralty notices. I did this work conscientiously and with a sense of responsibility; but it was not in the nature of things that I should ever recapture the excitement of that entry of Tanganyika on the blank of my old atlas.

It must not be supposed that I gave up my interest in the polar regions. My heart and my warm partici- pation swung from the frigid to the torrid zone, fasci- nated by the problems of each, no doubt, but more yet by the men who, like masters of a great art, worked each according to his temperament to complete the picture of the earth. Almost each day of my schoolboy life had its hour given up to their company. And to this day I think that it was a very good company.

Not the least interesting part in the study of geo- graphical discovery lies in the insight it gives one into the characters of that special kind of men who devoted the best part of their lives to the exploration of land and sea. In the world of mentality and imagination which I was entering it was they and not the characters of famous fiction who were my first friends. Of some of them I had soon formed for myself an image indissolubly connected with certain parts of the world. For instance, western Sudan, of which I could draw the rivers and principal features from memory even now, means for me an episode in Mungo Park's life.

It means for me the vision of a young, emaciated, fair-haired man, clad simply in a tattered shirt and worn-out breeches, gasping painfully for breath and lying on the ground in the shade of an enormous African tree (species unknown), while from a neighbouring village of grass huts a charitable black-skinned woman is approaching him with a calabash full of pure cold water, a simple draught which, according to himself, seems to have effected a miraculous cure. The central Sudan, on the other hand, is represented to me by a very different picture, that of a self-confident and keen- eyed person in a long cloak and wearing a turban on

his head, riding slowly towards a gate in the mud walls
of an African city, from which an excited population is
streaming out to behold the wonder—Doctor Barth,
the protégé of Lord Palmerston, and subsidized by the
British Foreign Office, approaching Kano, which no
European eye had seen till then, but where forty years
later my friend Sir Hugh Clifford, the Governor of
Nigeria, travelled in state in order to open a college.

I must confess that I read that bit of news and
inspected the many pictures in the illustrated papers
without any particular elation. Education is a great
thing, but Doctor Barth gets in the way. Neither will
the monuments left by all sorts of empire builders sup-
press for me the memory of David Livingstone. The
words "Central Africa" bring before my eyes an old man
with a rugged, kind face and a clipped, gray moustache,
pacing wearily at the head of a few black followers
along the reed-fringed lakes towards the dark native
hut on the Congo headwaters in which he died, clinging
in his very last hour to his heart's unappeased desire
for the sources of the Nile.

That passion had changed him in his last days from
a great explorer into a restless wanderer refusing to go
home any more. From his exalted place among the
blessed of militant geography and with his memory
enshrined in Westminster Abbey, he can well afford to
smile without bitterness at the fatal delusion of his
exploring days, a notable European figure and the most
venerated perhaps of all the objects of my early geographical enthusiasm.

Once only did that enthusiasm expose me to the
derision of my schoolboy chums. One day, putting my
finger on a spot in the very middle of the then white
heart of Africa, I declared that some day I would go
there. My chums' chaffing was perfectly justifiable.

I myself was ashamed of having been betrayed into mere vapouring. Nothing was further from my wildest hopes. Yet it is a fact that, about eighteen years afterwards, a wretched little stern-wheel steamboat I commanded lay moored to the bank of an African river.

Everything was dark under the stars. Every other white man on board was asleep. I was glad to be alone on deck, smoking the pipe of peace after an anxious day. The subdued thundering mutter of the Stanley Falls hung in the heavy night air of the last navigable reach of the Upper Congo, while no more than ten miles away, in Reshid's camp just above the Falls, the yet unbroken power of the Congo Arabs slumbered uneasily. Their day was over. Away in the middle of the stream, on a little island nestling all black in the foam of the broken water, a solitary little light glimmered feebly, and I said to myself with awe, "This is the very spot of my boyish boast."

A great melancholy descended on me. Yes, this was the very spot. But there was no shadowy friend to stand by my side in the night of the enormous wilderness, no great haunting memory, but only the unholy recollection of a prosaic newspaper "stunt" and the distasteful knowledge of the vilest scramble for loot that ever disfigured the history of human conscience and geographical exploration. What an end to the idealized realities of a boy's daydreams! I wondered what I was doing there, for indeed it was only an unforeseen episode, hard to believe in now, in my seaman's life. Still, the fact remains that I have smoked a pipe of peace at midnight in the very heart of the African continent, and felt very lonely there.

But never so at sea. There I never felt lonely, because there I never lacked company. The company of great navigators, the first grown-up friends of my early boyhood. The unchangeable sea preserves for one the sense of its past, the memory of things accomplished by wisdom and daring among its restless waves. It was those things that commanded my profoundest loyalty, and perhaps it is by the professional favour of the great navigators ever present to my memory that, neither explorer nor scientific navigator, I have been permitted to sail through the very heart of the old Pacific mystery, a region which even in my time remained very imperfectly charted and still remote from the knowledge of men.

It was in 1888, when in command of a ship loading in Sydney a mixed cargo for Mauritius, that, one day, all of a sudden, all the deep-lying historic sense of the exploring adventures in the Pacific surged up to the surface of my being. Almost without reflection I sat down and wrote a letter to my owners suggesting that, instead of the usual southern route, I should take the ship to Mauritius by way of Torres Strait. I ought to have received a severe rap on the knuckles, if only for wasting their time in submitting such an unheard-of proposition.

I must say I awaited the reply with some trepidation. It came in due course, but instead of beginning with the chiding words, "We fail to understand," etc., etc., it simply called my attention in the first paragraph to the fact that "there would be an additional insurance premium to pay for that route," and so on, and so on. And it ended like this: "Upon the whole, however, we have no objection to your taking the ship through Torres Strait if you are certain that the season is not too far advanced to endanger the success of your passage by the calms which, as you know, prevail at times in the Arafura Sea."

I read, and in my heart I felt compunctious. The season was somewhat advanced. I had not been scrupulously honest in my argumentation. Perhaps it was because I never expected it to be effective. And here it was all left to my responsibility. My letter must have struck a lucky day in Messrs. H. Simpson & Sons' offices—a romantic day. I won't pretend that I regret my lapse from strict honesty, for what would the memory of my sea life have been for me if it had not included a passage through Torres Strait, in its fullest extent, from the mouth of the great Fly River right on along the track of the early navigators.

The season being advanced, I insisted on leaving Sydney during a heavy southeast gale. Both the pilot and the tug-master were scandalized by my obstinacy, and they hastened to leave me to my own devices while still inside Sydney Heads. The fierce southeaster caught me up on its wings, and no later than the ninth day I was outside the entrance of Torres Strait, named after the undaunted and reticent Spaniard who, in the seventeenth century, first sailed that way without knowing where he was, without suspecting he had New Guinea on one side of him and the whole solid Australian continent on the other—he thought he was passing through an archipelago—the Strait whose existence for a century and a half had been doubted, argued about, squabbled over by geographers, and even denied by the disreputable but skilful navigator, Abel Tasman, who thought it was a large bay, and whose true contours were first laid down on the map by James Cook, the navigator without fear and without reproach, the greatest in achievement and character of the later seamen fathers of militant geography. If the dead haunt the scenes of their earthly exploits, then I must have been attended benevolently by those three shades—the inflexible Spaniard of such lofty spirit that in his report he disdains to say a single word about the appalling hardships and dangers of his passage; the pig-headed Hollander who, having made up his mind that there was no passage there, missed the truth by only fifty miles or so; and the great Englishman, a son of the soil, a great commander and a great professional seaman, who solved that question among many others and left no unsolved problems of the Pacific behind him. Great shades! All friends of my youth!

It was not without a certain emotion that, command-ing very likely the first, and certainly the last, merchant ship that carried a cargo that way—from Sydney to Mauritius—I put her head at daybreak for Bligh's Entrance, and packed on her every bit of canvas she could carry. Windswept, sunlit empty waters were all around me, half-veiled by a brilliant haze. The first thing that caught my eye upon the play of green white-capped waves was a black speck marking conveniently the end of a low sandbank. It looked like the wreck of some small vessel.

I altered the course slightly in order to pass close, with the hope of being able to read the letters on her stern. They were already faded. Her name was *Honolulu*. The name of the port I could not make out. The story of her life is known by now to God alone, and the winds must have drifted long ago around her remains a quiet grave of the very sand on which she had died. Thirty-six hours afterwards, of which about nine were spent at anchor, approaching the other end of the Strait, I sighted a gaunt, gray wreck of a big American ship lying high and dry on the southernmost of the Warrior Reefs. She had been there for years. I had heard of her. She was legendary. She loomed up, a sinister and enormous *memento mori* raised by the refraction of this serene afternoon above the far-away line of the horizon drawn under the sinking sun.

And thus I passed out of Torres Strait before the dusk settled on its waters. Just as a clear sun sank ahead of my ship I took a bearing of a little island for a fresh departure, an insignificant crumb of dark earth, lonely, like an advanced sentinel of that mass of broken land and water, to watch the approaches from the side of the Arafura Sea. But to me it was a hallowed spot, for I knew that the *Endeavour* had been hove to off it in the year 1762 for her captain, whose name was James Cook, to go ashore for half an hour. What he could possibly want to do I cannot imagine. Perhaps only to be alone with his thoughts for a moment. The dangers and the triumphs of exploration and discovery were over for that voyage. All that remained to do was to go home, and perhaps his great and equable soul, tempered in the incessant perils of a long exploration, wanted to commune with itself at the end of its task. It may be that on this dry crumb of the earth's crust which I was setting by compass he had tasted a moment of perfect peace. I could depict to myself the famous seaman navigator, a lonely figure in a three-cornered hat and square-skirted laced coat, pacing to and fro slowly on the rocky shore, while in the ship's boat, lying off on her oars, the coxswain kept his eyes open for the slightest sign of the captain's hand.

Thus the sea has been for me a hallowed ground, thanks to those books of travel and discovery which have peopled it with unforgettable shades of the masters in the calling which, in a humble way, was to be mine, too; men great in their endeavour and in hard-won successes of militant geography; men who went forth each according to his lights and with varied motives, laudable or sinful, but each bearing in his breast a spark of the sacred fire.

THE *TORRENS:* A PERSONAL TRIBUTE

I⊤ is one of the pleasant surprises of my accumulated years to be still here when the shade of that beautiful ship is being evoked for a moment by a sea-travel magazine before the eyes of a public which does its sea travelling under very different conditions. Personally I cannot help thinking them not so much improved as needlessly sophisticated. However, that opinion of mine may be wildly wrong. I am not familiar with the demands of the spirit of the age. And, besides, I know next to nothing of sea travel. Even of the people who do that thing I know but few. My two years in the *Torrens* is my only professional experience of passengers; and though we—officers brought up in strenuous Indiamen and famous wool clippers— did not think much of passengers, regarding them as derogatory nuisances with delicate feelings which prevented one driving one's ship till all was blue, I will confess that this experience was most fortunate from every point of view, marking the end of my sea life with pleasant memories, new impressions, and precious friendships. The pleasant memories include the excellent ship's companies it was my luck to work with on each of my two voyages. But the *Torrens* had a fame which attracted the right kind of sailor, and when engaging her crew her chief officer had always a large and promising crowd to pick and choose from. There was in it always a certain proportion of men who had served in her before and were anxious to join again; for apart from her more brilliant qualities, such as her speed and her celebrated good looks (which by themselves go a long way with a sailor), she was regarded as a "comfortable ship" in a strictly professional sense, which means that she was known to handle easily and to be a good sea boat in heavy weather. I cannot say that during my time in her we ever experienced really heavy weather; but we had the usual assortment of winds, up to "very strong gales" (logbook style), from various directions; and I can testify that, on every point of sailing, the way that ship had of letting big seas slip under her did one's heart good to watch. It resembled so much an exhibition of intelligent grace and unerring skill that it could fascinate even the least seamanlike of our passengers. A passage under sail brings out in the course of days whatever there may be of sea love and sea sense in any individual whose soul is not indissolubly wedded to the pedestrian shore.

There are, of course, degrees of landsmanism—even to the incurable. A gentleman whom we had on board on my first voyage presented an extreme instance of it. It, however, trenched upon the morbid in its excessive sea fright, which had its pathetic as well as comic moments. We had not been more than ten days out from Plymouth when he took it into his head that his shattered constitution could not stand the voyage. Note that he had not had as much as an hour of seasickness. He maintained, however, that a few more days at sea would certainly kill him. He was absolutely certain of it, and he pleaded day after day with a persistent agonized earnestness to be put ashore on the first convenient bit of land, which in this case would have been Teneriffe. But it is not so easy for a sailing ship to make an unexpected call without losing much time. Any deviation from a direct course of the voyage (unless in case of actual distress) would have invalidated the ship's insurance. It was not to be thought of, especially as the man looked fit enough and the doctor had reported that he could not find the slightest evidence of organic disease of any sort. I was sorry for my captain. He could not refuse to listen to the man. Neither could he accede to his request. It was absurd. And yet! . . . who could tell? It became worse when he began to offer progressive bribes up to £300 or more. I don't know why I was called to one of those awful conferences. The even, low flow of argument from those trembling lips impressed me. He exhibited to us his bank passbook to prove that he had the means to buy his life from us. Our doctor stood by in grim silence. The captain looked dead-tired, but kept his temper wonderfully under the implication of callous heartlessness. It was I who could not stand the inconclusive anguish of the situation. It was not so long since I had been neurasthenic myself. At the very next pause I remarked in a loud and cheery tone, "I suppose I had better get the anchors ready first thing to-morrow." The captain glared at me speechlessly, as well he might. But the effect of the hopeful word "anchors" had an instantaneous soothing effect on our passenger. As if satisfied that there was at last somebody on his side he was willing to leave it at that. He went out.

I need not say that next day the anchors were not touched. But we sighted Teneriffe at thirty miles off, to windward—a towering and majestic shadow against the sky. Our passenger spent the day leaning over the rail, watching it till it melted away in the dusk. It was the confirmation of a death sentence for him, I suppose. He took it very well.

He gave me the opportunity to admire for many days an exhibition of consistent stoicism. He never repined.

He withdrew within himself. Though civil enough when addressed directly, he had very few words to give to anybody—as though his fund of speech had been expended while pleading in vain for his life. But his heart was burning with indignant anger. He went ashore unreadable but unforgiving, without taking notice of any one in the ship. I was the only exception. Poor futile creature as I was, he remembered that I at least had seemed to be "on his side." If I may take an Irishman's privilege, I will say that if he had really died he could not have abhorred the ship and everyone in her more. To have been exposed to live for seventy days under a sentence of death was a soul-searing outrage, and he very properly resented it to the last.

I must say that, in general, our passengers would begin very soon to look thoroughly at home in the ship. Its life was homely enough and far removed from the ideals of the Ritz Hotel. The monotony of the sea is easier to bear than the boredom of the shore, if only because there is no visible remedy and no contrasts at hand to keep discontent alive. The world contains, or contained then, some people who could put up with a sense of peace for three months. The feeling of close confinement in a sailing ship, with her propelling power working in the open air, and with her daily life going on in public sight, and presenting the varied interests of human character and individual exertion, is always less oppressive than in a steamer even many times her size. Besides, in a sailing ship there are neither vibration nor mechanical noises to grow actively wearisome. Another advantage was that the sailing passenger ships of that epoch were never crowded. The cabins of the *Torrens* had two berths each, but they were roomy and not overfurnished with all sorts of inadequate contrivances for comfort, so-called. I have seen the cabins of a modern passenger steamship with three or four berths (their very couches being numbered) which were not half as big as ours. Not half as big—in fact, some of our passengers, who seized the opportunity of learning to dance the hornpipe from our boatswain (an agile professor), could pursue their studies in their own rooms. And that art requires for its practice more space than the proverbial swinging of a cat, I can assure you. Much more.

The *Torrens* was launched in 1875, only a few months after I had managed, after lots of trouble, to launch myself on the waters of the Mediterranean. Thus we began our careers about the same time. From the professional point of view hers was by far the greater success. It began early, and went on growing for fifteen years under the command of Captain H. R. Angell, whose own long career as a ship master was the greatest success of the three. He left her in 1890, and people said that he took his ship's luck away with him. The *Torrens* certainly lost some of her masts the very next voyage, by one of those sudden accidents for which no man can be made responsible. I joined her a year afterwards, on the 2d of November, 1891, in London, and I ceased to "belong to her," as the saying is (it was a wrench), on the 15th of October, 1893, when, in London Dock, I took a long look from the quay at that last of ships I ever had under my care, and, stepping round the corner of a tall warehouse, parted from her for ever, and at the same time stepped (in merciful ignorance) out of my sea life altogether.

I owed the opportunity of my close association with my famous contemporary to my acquaintance with Captain W. H. Cope, who succeeded Captain H. R. Angell. I had known him some years before, but only slightly, in a social way. I knew that he had been a

Conway boy, that he had had much varied service in
mail boats and in the Hooghly pilot steamer before the
command of the *Torrens* came in his way. But I had
no reason to believe that he remembered me particularly. However, on hearing from his brother that I
was ashore, he sent me word that the *Torrens* wanted
a chief officer, as a matter that might interest me. I
was then recovering slowly from a bad breakdown,
after a most unpleasant and persistent tropical disease
which I had caught in Africa while commanding a
steamer on the River Congo. Yet the temptation
was great. I confessed to him my doubts of my fitness
for the post, from the point of view of health. But he
said that moping ashore never did any one any good, and
was very encouraging. It was clear that, as the saying
goes, "my looks did not pity me," for he argued that,
so far as appearance went, there did not seem to be
anything the matter with me. And I suppose I could
never have been half as neurasthenic as our poor passenger who wanted to be put ashore, for I lasted out
for two voyages, as my discharges prove, though Mr.
Basil Lubbock, in his book, "The Colonial Clippers,"
credits me with only one. But in the end I had to go
(and even stay) ashore. Thus my famous contemporary outlived me at sea by many years, and if she had
perhaps a harder life of it than I, it was at least untinged
with unavailing regrets; and she escaped the ignomini-
ous fate of being laid up as a coal hulk, which so many
of her sisters had to suffer. Mr. Lubbock, who can put
so much interesting knowledge and right feeling into
his studies of our merchant ships, calls her "The Wonderful *Torrens*." She was! Her fascinations and virtues have made their marks on the hearts of men.
Only last year I received a letter from a young able
seaman, whom I remembered having in my watch,

invoking confidently her unforgotten name. "I feel sure you must be Mr. Conrad, the chief officer, in whose watch I was when serving in the *Torrens* in 1891, and so I venture to write to you. . . ." A friendly, quiet, middle-aged seaman's letter, which gave me the greatest pleasure. And I know of a retired sailor (a Britisher, I suppose), in Massachusetts, who is making a model in loving memory of her who, all her life, was so worthy of men's loyal service. I am sorry I had no time to go to see him, and to gaze at the pious work of his hands.

It is touching to read in Mr. Lubbock's book that, after her transfer to the Italian flag, when she was taken to Genoa to be broken up, the Genoese shipwrights were so moved by the beauty of her lines and the perfections of her build that they had no heart to break her up. They went to work instead to preserve her life for a few more years. A true labour of love, if ever there was one!

But in the end her body of iron and wood, so fair to look upon, had to be broken up—I hope with fitting reverence; and as I sit here, thirty years, almost to a day, since I last set eyes on her, I love to think that her perfect form found a merciful end on the shores of the sunlit sea of my boyhood's dreams, and that her fine spirit has returned to dwell in the regions of the great winds, the inspirers and the companions of her swift, renowned, sea-tossed life, which I, too, have been permitted to share for a little while.

CHRISTMAS DAY AT SEA

THEOLOGICALLY Christmas Day is the greatest occasion for rejoicing offered to sinful mankind; but this aspect of it is so august and so great that the human mind refuses to contemplate it steadily, perhaps because of its own littleness, for which of course it is in no way to blame. It prefers to concentrate its attention on ceremonial observances, expressive generally of good will and festivity, such, for instance, as giving presents and eating plum-puddings. It may be said at once here that from that conventional point of view the spirit of Christmas Day at sea appears distinctly weak. The opportunities, the materials too, are lacking. Of course, the ship's company get a plum-pudding of some sort, and when the captain appears on deck for the first time the officer of the morning watch greets him with a "Merry Christmas, sir," in a tone only moderately effusive. Anything more would be, owing to the difference in station, not correct. Normally he may expect a return for this in the shape of a "The same to you" of a nicely graduated heartiness. He does not get it always, however.

One Christmas morning, many years ago (I was young then and anxious to do the correct thing), my conventional greeting was met by a grimly scathing "Looks like it, doesn't it?" from my captain. Nothing more. A three-days' more or less thick weather had turned frankly into a dense fog, and I had him called according to orders. We were in the chops of the Channel, with the Scilly Islands on a vague bearing within thirty miles of us, and not a breath of wind anywhere. There the ship remained wrapped up in a damp blanket and as motionless as a post stuck right in the way of the wretched steamboats groping blindly in and out of the Channel. I felt I had behaved tactlessly; yet how rude it would have been to have withheld the season's greetings from my captain!

It is very difficult to know what is the right thing to do when one is young. I suffered exceedingly from my gaucherie; but imagine my disgust when in less than half an hour we had the narrowest possible escape from a collision with a steamer which, without the slightest warning sound, appeared like a vague dark blot in the fog on our bow. She only took on the shape of a ship as she passed within twenty yards of the end of our jibboom, terrifying us with the furious screeching of her whistle. Her form melted into nothing, long before the end of the beastly noise, but I hope that her people heard the simultaneous yell of execration from thirty-six throats which we sent after her by way of a Christmas greeting. Nothing more at variance with the spirit of peace and good will could be imagined; and I must add that I never saw a whole ship's company get so much affected by one of the "close calls" of the sea. We remained jumpy all the morning and consumed our Christmas puddings at noon with restless eyes and straining ears as if under the shadow of some impending marine calamity or other.

On shore, of course, a calamity at Christmas time would hardly take any other shape than that of an avalanche—avalanche of unpaid bills. I think that it is the absence of that kind of danger which makes Christmas at sea rather agreeable on the whole. An additional charm consists in there being no worry about presents. Presents ought to be unexpected things.

The giving and receiving of presents at appointed times seems to me a hypocritical ceremony, like exchanging gifts of Dead Sea fruit in proof of sham good-fellowship. But the sea of which I write here is a live sea; the fruits one chances to gather on it may be salt as tears or bitter as death, but they never taste like ashes in the mouth.

In all my twenty years of wandering over the restless waters of the globe I can only remember one Christmas Day celebrated by a present given and received. It was, in my view, a proper live-sea transaction, no offering of Dead Sea fruit; and in its unexpectedness perhaps worth recording. Let me tell you first that it happened in the year 1879, long before there was any thought of wireless messages, and when an inspired person trying to prophesy broadcasting would have been regarded as a particularly offensive nuisance and probably sent to a rest-cure home. We used to call them madhouses then, in our rude, cave-man way.

The daybreak of Christmas Day in the year 1879 was fine. The sun began to shine sometime about four o'clock over the sombre expanse of the Southern Ocean in latitude 51; and shortly afterwards a sail was sighted ahead. The wind was light, but a heavy swell was running. Presently I wished a "Merry Christmas" to my captain. He looked still sleepy, but amiable. I reported the distant sail to him and ventured the opinion that there was something wrong with her. He said, "Wrong?" in an incredulous tone. I pointed out that she had all her upper sails furled and that she was brought to the wind, which, in that region of the world, could not be accounted for on any other theory. He took the glasses from me, directed them towards her stripped masts resembling three Swedish safety matches, flying up and down and waggling to and fro ridiculously in that heaving and austere wilderness of countless water-hills, and returned them to me without a word. He only yawned. This marked display of callousness gave me a shock. In those days I was generally inexperienced and still a comparative stranger in that particular region of the world of waters.

The captain, as is a captain's way, disappeared from the deck; and after a time our carpenter came up the poop ladder carrying an empty small wooden keg, of the sort in which certain ship's provisions are packed. I said, surprised, "What do you mean by lugging this thing up here, Chips?"—"Captain's orders, sir," he explained shortly.

I did not like to question him further, and so we only exchanged Christmas greetings and he went away. The next person to speak to me was the steward. He came running up the companion stairs: "Have you any old newspapers in your room, sir?"

We had left Sydney, N.S.W., eighteen days before. There were several old Sydney *Heralds*, *Telegraphs*, *Bulletins* in my cabin, besides a few home papers received by the last mail. "Why do you ask, steward?" I inquired naturally. "The captain would like to have them," he said.

And even then I did not understand the inwardness of these eccentricities. I was only lost in astonishment at them. It was eight o'clock before we had closed with that ship, which, under her short canvas and heading nowhere in particular, seemed to be loafing aimlessly on the very threshold of the gloomy home of storms. But long before that hour I had learned from the number of the boats she carried that this nonchalant ship was a whaler. She was the first whaler I had ever seen. She had hoisted the Stars and Stripes at her peak, and her signal flags had told us already that her name was: "*Alaska*—two years out from New York—east from Honolulu—two hundred and fifteen days on the cruising ground."

We passed, sailing slowly, within a hundred yards of her; and just as our steward started ringing the breakfast bell the captain and I held aloft, in good view of the figures watching us over her stern, the keg, properly headed up and containing, besides an enormous bundle of old newspapers, two boxes of figs in honour of the day. We flung it far out over the rail. Instantly our ship, sliding down the slope of a high swell, left it far behind in our wake. On board the *Alaska* a man in a fur cap flourished an arm; another, a much be-whiskered person, ran forward suddenly. I never saw anything so ready and so smart as the way that whaler, rolling desperately all the time, lowered one of her boats. The Southern Ocean went on tossing the two ships like a juggler his gilt balls, and the microscopic white speck of the boat seemed to come into the game instantly, as if shot out from a catapult on the enormous and lonely stage. That Yankee whaler lost not a moment in picking up her Christmas present from the English wool clipper.

Before we had increased the distance very much she dipped her ensign in thanks and asked to be reported "All well, with a catch of three fish." I suppose it paid them for two hundred and fifteen days of risk and toil, away from the sounds and sights of the inhabited world, like outcasts devoted, beyond the confines of mankind's life, to some enchanted and lonely penance.

Christmas Days at sea are of varied character, fair to middling and down to plainly atrocious. In this statement I do not include Christmas Days on board

passenger ships. A passenger is, of course, a brother
(or sister), and quite a nice person in a way, but his
Christmas Days are, I suppose, what he wants them
to be: the conventional festivities of an expensive
hotel included in the price of his ticket.

OCEAN TRAVEL

THE one statement that can safely be advanced about travelling at sea is that it is not what it used to be. It is different now elementally. It is not so much a matter of changed propelling power; it is something more. In the old days, under the machinery of sails, the distinguished and the undistinguished travellers (of whom there were not so very many) were wafted to distant parts of the world by the movement of variable air currents. Now the travelling multitudes are taken to their destination because of the invariable resistance of water to the screwing motion of the propeller, with which fire (that other element) has a lot to do. The whole affair of progress across the seas has become much more complicated and much more precise on its physical side. It has grown also into a marvel.

But a marvellous achievement is not necessarily interesting. It may render life more tame than perhaps it should be. I do not mean that any marvel of applied science can tame the wild spirit that lurks in all men, and of which the proofs are not far to seek. It only makes the condition of our pilgrimage less exciting.

The whole psychology of sea travel is changed. Formerly a man setting out on a sea voyage broke away from shore conditions and found in the ship a new kind of home. This applied even to such comparatively short passages as across the Atlantic. But now a man (especially if setting out for the United States) brings the conditions of shore life with him on board, and finds in his ship the usual sort of hotel, with its attempts at all kinds of sham comforts, all the disadvantages of gregarious life, with the added worry of not being able to get away from it for a certain number of days. The only comfort is to be found in the assurance that the number of days is not great and that, barring accidents, it is fixed. There is a definite date to look forward to—the date of release from that more or less luxurious prison any ship must be to any passenger.

That every passenger (even in the biggest and most hotel-like Atlantic ferries with their territorial names) wishes to escape there can be not the slightest doubt. He may say what he likes, but it is a fact of human nature. He looks forward to his release much as any prisoner. The modern traveller has never the time to get into an acquiescent mood. The sham shore conditions which the shipping companies try to create for him stand in the way, too. The hold of the land (which is his natural element) is on him all through the passage, and he suffers from a subtle disharmony between his natural tastes and his surroundings.

It was otherwise with the old-time traveller under sail: he had to become acclimatized to that moral atmosphere of ship life which he was fated to breathe for so many days. He was no dweller in an unpleasantly unsteady imitation of a Ritz Hotel. He would before long begin to feel himself a citizen of a small community in special conditions and with special interests which gradually ceased to be secret to him, and in the end secured his sympathies. The machinery of his propulsion, the picturesque activities of the men of the sea, lay open to his sight and appealed to his sympathies.

In the course of my sea life, a time when it never occurred to me that I myself might be a passenger some day, I was for a couple of years officer of a sailing passenger ship out of the Port of London. This gave me the opportunity to watch that process of acclimatization of which I have spoken, in a group of about sixty persons of various ages and temperaments, some travelling for their health and others only for rest—which they indubitably secured in our passages that averaged about eighty days. Part of our passengers, those from the Midlands generally, used to come on board in London Dock, while others, those from the South and from London itself preferred to join the ship in Plymouth, where we had to call in order to embark the live stock for the voyage. Of that feathered and four-footed company the most important item was the milch-cow which joined the ship mainly "for the benefit of the children," as the advertisements had it. It was the last living thing that came on board, already boxed and in its travelling stall, and displaying a most praiseworthy composure even while spinning in midair at the foreyard arm before being landed on the foredeck against the mast, to which its straitened habitation was secured for the passage with lashings of chain and rope fit to withstand the heaviest weather we were likely to encounter.

There, on fine mornings (and there are more fine mornings at sea than have ever been dreamt of in a landsman's philosophy), the ship's children, some controlled by nursemaids, others running loose, trooped forward to pay a visit to their cow, which looked with mild big eyes at the small citizens of our sea community with the air of knowing all there was to know about them.

All this may sound very primitive, but it had a charm and an intimacy of a settled existence no modern steamship with its long barren alleyways swept by the wind and decorated with the name of promenade decks can give. The modern passenger may be able to walk a good many miles in his ship in the course of the day, but this is the only thing which differentiates him from the bales of goods carried in the hold—this, and the power of swallowing the food which is presented to him at regular intervals. He is carried along swiftly and fed delicately, but the other lived the life of his ship, that sort of life which is not sustained on bread (and *suprême au volaille*) alone, but depends for its interest on enlarged sympathies and awakened perceptions of nature and men.

I have seen old maiden ladies develop during a passage nice discrimination in the matter of steering. They had their favourite helmsmen. Elderly business men would become good judges of the set of the sails and acquire a seaman's eye for the aspects of the weather—and almost all, men and women, became reconciled to the vast solitude of the sea untroubled by the sound of the world's mechanical contrivances and the noise of its endless controversies. The silence of the universe would lie very close to the sailing ship, with her freight of lives from which the daily stresses and anxieties had been removed, as if the circle of the horizon had been a magic ring laid on the sea. No doubt the days thus enchanted were empty, but they were not so tedious as people may imagine. They passed quickly, and, if they brought no profit or excitement, I cannot help thinking that they were not wasted. No! They were not wasted.

OUTSIDE LITERATURE

HAVING been prompted by a certain literary suggestion to reflect upon the nature of Notices to Mariners, I fell to examining some of my old feelings and impressions which, strictly professional as they were, have yet contributed in the end towards the existence of a certain amount of literature; or at any rate of pages of prose. The Notices to Mariners are good prose but I think no critic would admit them into the body of literature. And it is only as compositions in prose that I believe myself competent to speak of them. And first let me thank God that they do not belong to imaginative literature. It would be dreadful if they did. An imaginatively written Notice to Mariners would be a deadly thing. I mean it literally. It would be sure to kill a number of people before its imaginative quality had been appreciated and suppressed. That their style must be clear and concise, and the punctuation of the ordinary kind, would not necessarily militate against their being regarded as literature. The Maxims of La Rochefoucauld are concise enough. But they open horizons; they plumb the depths; they make us squirm, shudder, smile in turn; and even sigh—at times; whereas the prose of the Notices to Mariners must do nothing of the kind.

And it doesn't. A mariner detected shuddering or sighing over a Notice to Mariners would simply (to speak in unliterary language) be not fit for his job. All means of acting on man's spiritual side are forbidden

to that prose. In those compositions which are read
as earnestly as anything that ever came from printing
press, all suggestion of Love, of Adventure, of Romance,
of Speculation, of all that decorates and ennobles life,
except Responsibility, is barred. What we expect
from them is not suggestion but information of an
ideal accuracy, such as you do not find in the prose
of the works on science, which is mainly imaginative
and often solemnly mystifying. That is why some
quite decent men are moved to smile as they read it.
But there is no mystification in the language of truth
contained in the Notices to Mariners. You would not
want to smile at them. No decent man would. Even
Mr. Punch, to whom as a great burlesque poet nothing
is supposed to be sacred, and who has been seen lately
taking liberties with the explosive atom, would not
dream of making fun out of Notices to Mariners. Mr.
Punch knows better. He knows that for an inspired
poet who sees the mystic relations of sublunary matters, Notices to Mariners are things to be read rev-
erently. They are like declarations of a minutely
careful Providence. They can be imagined as dictated
in a quiet voice by the angel who, in the words of the
song, sits aloft to watch over poor Jack. They belong
to a prose which, if certainly not immortal, is revelatory
to its own generation.

Addressed to a special public, limited to a very
definite special subject, having no connection with the
intellectual culture of mankind, and yet of some importance to a civilization which is founded on the protection of life and property, that prose has only one
ideal to attain, to hold on to: the ideal of perfect
accuracy. You would say that such an ideal may easily
be captured by a steady, prosaic mind devoting itself
for a few minutes (the Notices to Mariners are short)

every day to the task of composition. Why, yes! But what about misprints—the bane of authors?

And then the absences. I mean the absences of mind. It is a fact that the most pedestrian mind will sometimes take a flight from the office where it works (I suppose Notices to Mariners are written in some sort of office) toward subjects of poetic fancy, its children, its lady love, its glass of beer, and such other things interesting to its mortal envelope. I often wondered what the author of Notices to Mariners looks like. I have tried to represent him to myself as a monk, a man who has renounced the vanities of the world, and for preference belonging to the order of Trappists who are bidden to remember death—*memento mori*—and nothing else. A sobering thought! Just suppose the author of Notices to Mariners acquiring convivial habits and sitting down to write a Notice in that happy frame of mind when nothing matters much and one letter of the alphabet is as good as another. For myself—who am not convivial in that sense and have written a varied lot of prose with a quite ridiculous scrupulosity and an absurd seriousness—I don't mind confessing that if I were told to write a Notice to Mariners I would not pray perhaps—for I have my own convictions about the abuse of prayer—but I would certainly fast. I would fast in the evening and get up to write my Notice to Mariners at four o'clock in the morning for fear of accidents. One letter is so soon written for another—with fatal results.

It happened to me many years ago to endanger the course of my humble career at sea simply by writing the letter W instead of the letter E at the bottom of a page full of figures. It was an examination and I ought to have been plucked mercilessly. But in consideration, I believe, of all my other answers being

correct I was handed that azimuth paper back by the
examiner's assistant, with the calm remark, "You have
fourteen minutes yet." I looked at the face of the
clock; it was round like the moon, white as a ghost,
unfeeling, idiotic. I sat down under it with the conviction of the crushing materiality of time, and calling
in my mind the assistant examiner a sarcastic brute.
For no man could have gone over all those figures in
fourteen minutes. I hope my exasperated consternation at this check could not be detected. It was funny
even to myself. Then, just at the moment when my
sinking heart had touched bottom, I saw the error
staring at me, enormous, gross, palpable. I traced
hastily a capital E over the W and went back to the
desk with my sheet of blue paper in a still shaky hand.
The assistant hardly glanced at it before he let it drop,
and I saw then that in my lack of comprehension it
was I who had been an unqualified brute. For in his
remark about the fourteen minutes he had clearly tried
to give me a hint. He was a charming young man,
obviously poor, with an intelligent, as if suffering, face.
Not exactly sickly, but delicate. A sea voyage would
have done him good. But it was I who went to sea
—this time bound to Calcutta.

And it was in Calcutta, a few months afterwards,
that one morning my captain on going ashore saw me
busy about the decks and beckoned to me in that way
ship masters have, or used to have. I mean ship masters who commanded their ships from truck to keelson
as it were, technically and spiritually, in motion and at
rest, and through every moment of their life, when the
seaman's calling was by the mere force of its conditions
more vocational than it can be at the present day.
My ship master had that way of beckoning. What
way? Well—all I can say of it is that one dropped

everything. I can't describe it better. So I dropped whatever I was doing and he said: "You will find a Notice on the cabin table. Go in and enter it on the proper Admiralty sheet. Do it now." Which I hastened to do.

That examination, the issue of which had hung on a capital letter, had caused me to be officially certified as fit to undertake that particular duty; and ever since then my familiarity with Notices to Mariners, which are not literature, went on growing through a course of years, up to the moment when stepping ashore for the last time I lost all touch with the most trusted kind of printed prose. Henceforth I had to begin (while totally unprovided with Notices to Authors) to write prose myself; and the pains I took with it only my Maker knows! And yet I never learned to trust it. I can't trust it to this day. We who write prose which is not that of the Notices to Mariners are forgotten by Providence. No angel watches us at our toil. A dreadful doubt hangs over the whole achievement of literature; I mean that of its greatest and its humblest men. Wasn't it "Papa Augier" who, being given a copy of "Hamlet," glanced through it expertly and then dropped it with the dry remark: "*Vous appelez ça une pièce, vous?*" The whole tragedy of art lies in the nutshell of this terrifying anecdote. But it never will occur to anybody to question the prosaic force of the author of Notices to Mariners, which are not literature, and his fidelity to his honourable ideal—the ideal of perfect accuracy.

LEGENDS

To watch the growth of a legend is a sad occupation. It is not so much because legends deal with people and things finished and done with; that they spring, as it were, from amongst the bones of dead men. Flowers (as I have seen myself) will do that too. That's all in the order of nature, and both flowers and legends are upon the whole decorative, which is all to the good.

I have nothing against a legend twining its tendrils fancifully about the facts of history or the tables of statistics (which can be fanciful too, though they can never be made very decorative). They spring from noble soil, they are a form of memory which we all like to leave behind us, that lingers about the achievement of men who have had their day and the vanished forms of things which have served the needs of their time.

One could welcome that fine form of imaginative recognition of the past with nothing worse than the gentle melancholy which the passage of time brings in its train if it were not disfigured by touches of fatuity of which no legend is wholly free, because I suspect that those who record its tales as picked out on the lips of men are doing it in a spirit of love. And that is only right and proper. But love is uncritical. It is an enthusiastic state seeing romance in what may be not true to the spirit of its subject, so to speak. And thus the false which is often fatuous also creeps into a worthy or even noble story.

Or even into a holy story. The Golden Legend itself. The legend of saints and their miracles is an awful example of that danger—as any one who turns over a few pages of it may see. Saintliness is made absurd by the presentation of the miraculous facts themselves. It lacks spirituality in a surprising way.

Yes, fatuity lurks in all legends fatally by the effect of our common credulity. However, the legend I have in my mind has nothing to do with saints—but with beings at first sight infinitely different, but whose lives were hard (no saint, I take it, ever slept on a bed of roses) if not exactly ascetic, and if not hermit-like, yet as far removed from the commonest amenities and the simplest affections which make life sweet, and as much removed from the material interests of this world as the most complete spiritual renunciation could make it.

Perhaps nobody could guess from what precedes that I have sailors in my mind. I do not mean to be irreverent if I insist that in a temporal sense there was much that was edifying in their lives. They did not work miracles, to be sure, but I have seen them repeatedly do all that men can do for their faith—if it was only the faith in their own manhood. And that is something, surely. But there was something more in it, something larger—a fidelity to the demands of their calling which I verily believe was for all of them I knew, both afloat and ashore, vocational quite as much in its way as any spiritual call a man's nature has ever responded to. And all that for no perceptible reward in the praise of man and the favour of gods—I mean the sea gods, an indigent, pitiless lot, who had nothing to offer to servants at their shrine but a ward in some hospital on shore or a sudden wedding with death in a great uproar, but with no gilding of fine words about it. *La mort sans phrases.*

In all this there is material for a fine legend, if not

of saintly virtues, then of a consistent display of manhood. And the legend will not be long, for the last days of sailing ships were short if one thinks of the countless ages since the first sail of leather or rudely woven rushes was displayed to the wind. Stretching the period both ways to the utmost, it lasted from 1850 to 1910. Just sixty years. Two generations. The winking of an eye. Hardly the time to drop a prophetic tear. For the pathos of that era lies in the fact that when the sailing ships and the art of sailing them reached their perfection, they were already doomed. It was a swift doom, but it is consoling to know that there was no decadence.

That era has, however, had its historians, such as Mr. Basil Lubbock, for instance, whose devotion to the glory of the ships and the merits of the men has the character of one of those romantic passions that last a lifetime. He is now of the brotherhood initiated with all the awful ceremonies of a Cape Horn passage. He speaks with much knowledge. And there is Miss C. Fox-Smith, in whom I verily believe the quintessence of the collective soul of the latter-day seaman has found its last resting-place and a poignant voice before taking its flight for ever from the earth. Truth itself speaks in her verse—I can safely say, since I (surprising thought) have one foot, at least, in that irrecoverable phase of old sea life for which their piety and their talents have done so much.

It is on that ground that I would remonstrate with Mr. Lubbock against the admission into one of his books of sea chronicles of a tale which would degrade the character of any legend. The facts of a legend need not be literally true. But they ought to be credible and they must be in a sort of fundamental accord with the nature of the life they record, that is with the char-

acter of their subject matter. The subject of the
Golden Legend is, in fact, the celebration of a miracle-
working holiness, and the subject of any sea legend
must be the celebration of the era of fair ships sailed
with consummate seamanship—an era that seems as
distant now as the age of miracles.

The history of the latter days of clipper ships and
their men may be said to begin with the *Marco Polo*
and the man who commanded her. His name was
Forbes, and he is not a figure to stand at the head of a
sea legend. He lacked balance in his character. Luck
alone made him, and at the first adversity he collapsed.
But without going into the details of his short career,
I am sure I am doing good service to his memory by
trying to purge his record of the most fatuous tale
that ever cropped up in any legend of the sea.

As adopted, alas! (but the best of us may err) by
Mr. Basil Lubbock, it runs that Forbes used to padlock
the sheets of the *Marco Polo's* sails—one reviewer ex-
plaining kindly "to guard against the timid members
of a crew," a priceless phrase, whatever it may mean.
What is a "timid member" and how do you recognize
him? Anyhow, I am sure he is a fitting person to play
his part in that padlock story.

I wonder who was the man to tell it? He must have
been an ironmonger trying for a new outlet for his
wares. And to what sort of audience? Personally I
would have been afraid to tell it to the Horse-Marines
—that mysterious corps which is famed for its capacity
to swallow anything in the way of a yarn.

[This article was left unfinished at Conrad's death.]

THE UNLIGHTED COAST

I CAME ashore bringing with me strongest of all, and most persistent, the impression of a great darkness. I do not mean darkness in a symbolic or spiritual sense. Indeed, one couldn't come from contact with the watchers of that darkness, and the workers therein, otherwise than spiritually strengthened. What I mean is the fact itself, the fact of darkness spread over the land and water of old civilization such as wrapped up early mariners' landfalls on their voyages of exploration. To him who had been accustomed to behold after long sea passages the shadowy contours of the English coast illuminated festally, interminably, unfailingly, as if for a sleepless feast or for sleepless toil, the impression was very powerful—like a revelation of some deeper truth. Fires in the night are the sign of mankind's life to an eye at sea. There were no such signs anywhere. Not a gleam. And yet life had never before perhaps in the history of that unlighted island known such an intense consciousness of itself. No! Life had not departed that sombre shore. It was only its old sense of security that was no longer there.

It had a strange air of finality. The land had turned to a shadow. Of all scourges and visitations against which mankind prays to Heaven, it was not pestilence that had smitten that shore dark; it was war; with sudden death, another of that dreaded company, full of purpose, in the air, on the water, and under the water. Breathing the calm air of the night, looking at this placid sea gleaming faintly, here and there, as

still water will do in the dark, it was as hard to believe
in the existence of this prowling death as in the daunt-
less, tense life of that obscured land. That mere
shadow—big with fate.

One seemed to have one's being in the very centre of
illusory appearance. The very silence, so profound
around us as to seem boundless, and harmonizing marvellously with the spirit of the hour, was not true to
the usual meaning it conveys to a human mind, that of
being cut off from communication with its kind.

For just as I was remarking to the officer by my
side that surely neither Cæsar's galleys nor the ships
of the Danish rovers had ever found on their approach
this land so absolutely and scrupulously lightless as
this—just then a voice behind us was heard: "I've
here two messages I have just picked up."

It was our wireless man. That shadow emitting
no sound waves, no waves of light, was talking to its
watchers at sea; filling the silence with words pregnant
with the truth, the naked, ugly truth of the situation.

And the man with two white pieces of paper very
noticeable in his hand said: "It's our station at X
speaking."

For reasons which had nothing to do with its effi-
cicency we could not use our wireless installation very
often, and he was immensely pleased at having picked
up something for the first time in two days. We went
below to de-code the messages. The little cabin, in
contrast with the variously shaded and toned darkness
we had left, seemed scandalously over-lighted.

Although I helped to de-code these messages I don't
remember the exact words of their concise phrases;
but the first was an inquiry, apparently directed at
large into space, relating to a hostile submarine seen
off the coast not many hours before. The other was

a request addressed by name to a ship at sea for a report on some floating mines discovered in a certain position within the last twenty-four hours. The great motionless shadow was talking to its watchers, small shadows flitting here and there on the obscure gleams of the smooth sea veiled in the unmoral night that from its very nature favours aggression rather than vigilance, without regard to the merits of the case.

These were good samples of the talk that flows on unheard in sunshine, in starlight, under the clouds. War talk. But how different from the war talk we hear on the lips of men (and even great men) which often seems but talk round the war, obscuring the one and only question: To be or not to be—the great alternative of an appeal to arms. The other, the grouped-letters war talk, almost without sound and altogether without fury, is full of sense, of meaning, and single-minded purpose; inquiries, information, orders, reports. Words, too. But words in direct relation to things and facts, with the feeling at the back of it all of the correct foresight that planned and of the determination which carries on the protective work.

We all know that a true defence is at the point of the sword; but the shield has its part to play too in defensive work. This work had been planned by the navy in anticipation of the conditions that would arise. I know that praise often is but more or less conscious impertinence. But, after all, this is seamen's work, and half a lifetime at sea may perhaps justify me in expressing the highest possible sense of the navy's clear-eyed foresight in planning, and the judgment, resolution, tact, and knowledge of men in getting the planned system to work, from the first critical days to its full development of to-day, steadily, without haste, yet with that speed which is inherent in the force, unswerving purpose, and in the resolute handling of any problem under the sun.

It is mainly the officers and men of the various branches of the R.N.R. who, under the high command of naval officers, have been entrusted with the manifold duties of that simple work of protection and watchfulness. It was the navy who trained them to it, and as the period had in each case to be short, the general efficiency with which the work is done speaks well for the naval method. But it is also a high testimony to the capacity, adaptability, and the whole-souled earnestness of the officers of the Merchant Service who hastened to join, some called up, others volunteering without hesitation from all the points of the compass and from the uttermost ends of the Empire.

Much has been said already of these men and of their activities; of the circumstances, the conditions, the incidents of the task. I may perhaps later say something too, more in the nature of a personal impression than of detailed description. As to the work itself, all I want to point out now is that seen from outside it presents in its various branches the aspect of a nerve-straining drudgery. And in that outward aspect there is a proportion of truth. From its very nature it must be work without glamour. No great moments can be expected in it. Yet, rare as drops of rain in a desert, such moments have been vouchsafed to some of the faithful. As I trace these words I have in my mind the most unexpected, the most unforeseen instance of the kind. An enormous drop in a parched and stress-ful monotony of duty.

On the morning I heard the tale, the pier at one of our "bases," with its central line of neat shed-like buildings and the great signal bridge at the end (recalling the superstructure of a battleship), had been for a moment swept clean of all life by a rain squall as effectually as by a point-blank broadside of shrapnel shell.

My companion and I took cover in the wardroom, a good-sized apartment lined with varnished match-boarding. A heavy table occupied the middle. The officer of the watch, a silent, detached figure, sat at a writing desk reading a note, while a young bluejacket, cap in hand, waited for the answer. Two R.N.R. officers smoking by the fire greeted us. Another sat at some distance on a chair placed against the wall near a window. He took no notice of our arrival.

But the officer with me murmured with a nod in his direction: "This is our Zeppelin-strafer."

I said: "No! Have you that, too, in your lot?"

"Yes. He'll tell you all about it."

I was introduced with a word or two of comment to "our Zeppelin-strafer." There was no halo around his head. He was young, so young that he must have belonged to the third generation of those who had gone to sea since my time; one of those who began that life after 1900. A seaman of the twentieth century! And yet he was no stranger to me. The memories of my twenty sea years crowded upon me, memories of faces, of temperaments, of expressions. And looking at him, all I could say to myself was:—How like! We sat down side by side near the window. He was in no haste to begin. He belonged to the shy, silent type —and how like!

It's an odious thing to have to write in "descriptive" fashion of men with whom one talked like a friend and had found acceptance as one of themselves. If he sees these lines I hope he will forgive me. It's very likely that my impressions set down truthfully are altogether untrue. We were but half an hour together, and when we parted and he closed the door of that room behind him I felt that he was as utterly gone from me as though he had stepped out in the middle of the Pacific.

He began to talk to me with a sort of reluctance, hesitatingly, till I mentioned to him that I had been to sea much longer than himself, if not so recently. He knew I was some sort of writing man, and was ready to be civil, but after that remark of mine his articulation became easier. Not much, though. He looked down on the ground, glancing at me only now and again, and spoke in a low tone with unexpected pauses. The best way in which I can characterize that narrative is by saying that he delivered it to me with the aspect, the bearing of a man who broods over the event in silence.

He was making his way on a foggy day back to his base after a spell of duty outside. His craft mounted one gun; and without going into unnecessary description I may best give an idea of the size of his command by saying that, when he was reposing, the breech of the gun was within four feet of his head as it lay on his pillow. For reasons that need not be stated, his vessel did not move then more than about three knots through the water—which was smooth. There's seldom much wind with thick weather. On that occasion there was a very light breeze, enough to help the fog at its usual pranks of thinning and thickening, opening and shutting, lifting in patches and closing down suddenly— quicker than a wink, sometimes.

He was walking up and down his vast deck when, turning aft, he saw the fore-end of a Zeppelin emerge into misty view out of an apparently thicker layer of fog. From then on for succeeding minutes he moved no more than a ship's timber. The apparition took

him completely unawares because he had not heard
any noise in the air before. Directly, however, he
caught sight of the Zeppelin he heard the noise of the
engine very plainly.

As soon as he regained the power of speech he uttered
the words "Action . . . Zeppelin . . . Astern,"
in a cautious whisper. An unnecessary precaution.
But he told me that at first the "enormous thing seemed
right on top of us!" In fact, it was not anything so
near as that. It was coming up astern but a little on
one side and, he noticed, steering a course which would
cross obliquely his wake and bring the monster very
close indeed—within 500 yards perhaps.

For whatever reason, it was flying low, so low that
he did not need to throw his head up much to watch
its steady progress. And there followed for him such
moments of unforgettable anguish, something like the
anguish of a man whose eternal salvation would depend
on the soundness of his judgment.

The problem was how to deal with this gigantic piece
of luck. For if he opened fire too soon the chances
were that the German would swerve and get away, or,
climbing overhead, would descend on him as low as he
pleased and bomb him out of existence. His gun was
a very good weapon of its kind, but it was not an anti-
aircraft gun and had only a limited amount of elevation.
And there was also the possibility that, utterly unconscious of the tiny speck lost in the shimmer of the thin
fog layer below, the Zeppelin would alter its course at
any moment for some purpose of its own.

What worried and discomposed him was the insistent
whispering of his skipper, who had crept to his elbow
and was entreating hoarsely not to waste a moment,
"to let the beggar have it now, sir. Let him have it."
The German meantime held on. Ordering the skipper

away he had the fortitude, though his heart was in his mouth all the time, to hold out till the Zeppelin crossed his wake and exposed the greater part of its side. . . . "And then," he said, "we started to plug it into him as fast as we could load. And every shot was a hit."

He looked at me with strangely troubled eyes. "It was impossible to miss . . . you know," he added in a lowered voice.

Whether conscious or unconscious before of the microscopic strafer below, Fritz must have had the surprise of his life. The record shock of Zeppelin history. His dismay was boundless, something very like panic up there became visible to the eyes below.

. . . "I could see three or four of them running along," went on the low voice. "I saw them quite plainly. If I had had half-a-dozen men with rifles on my deck we could have got every single one of them."

The Zeppelin swung off wide and with its engines working noisily, made off without more ado. Its own speed or the drift of denser fog blowing over turned it into a mere dark blur swiftly. As long as the faintest shadow of it remained visible the fire was kept up. Then it ceased. A profound silence ensued. It was all over. He was gone.

It was, however, possible that he might return overhead and take his revenge. But before the strafers on deck had the time to exchange glances of wonder, apprehension, or inquiry, while they were still, in fact, staring into the upper fog, the shadow reappeared nearer than before aslant in the white space, sliding downwards stern first, its nose tilted up at a perilous angle.

"Of course we opened on him instantly," he went on. "And do you know what he did then?"

At this point he looked at me again, and after a little

gasp went on, as if unwillingly, "he dumped all his bombs overboard. The whole lot of them at once."

The resulting explosion was something terrific. He felt as if his little craft were blown clean out of the water and at the same time hit by a tidal wave. And in the awful commotion, uproar, and black smoke the Zeppelin shot up and vanished for good.

"You must have made him very sick," I said.

"He looked very sick indeed," said the young strafer quietly.

"I wonder what became of him?"

"Hard to say. There was a report in the papers some time afterwards. . . . Damaged Zeppelin coming to the ground in Norway. . . . I sometimes think . . ."

He did not finish the sentence. He had been eighteen months of long days and longer nights at his protecting work, out and in, fair or foul, never seeing anything to reward his strained, hopeful vigilance, and sometimes for days seeing nothing at all. For the North Sea is a big place, as our coasters say: so big that there may be half-a-dozen ships out looking for you because you are a little late in returning (as it happened to a man), and you will come in innocently, having seen no one, unseen by anybody—which is vexing for the anxious searchers.

Eighteen patient, unfaltering months, and then this ten gloriously crowded minutes—is that much? The whole affair probably did not last so long.

Rare, like drops of water in a desert, are such opportunities for the watchers of the lightless shore. And to this one Fortune had not been fickle, but simply outrageous. The drop had merely brushed past his lips so unskilled in speech. He had talked to me in all friendliness, for which I am duly grateful; yet he left me with the impression that had he been permitted to taste the full flavour, his official report would have remained, of his own choice, his first and last utterance. I fancy, somehow, that rather than talk of luck so immense that there could be no fit words for it in the world, he would have preferred to brood over it in adequate silence.

THE DOVER PATROL

THE worth of a sentiment lies in the sacrifices men will make for its sake. All ideals are built on the ground of solid achievement, which in a given profession creates in the course of time a certain tradition, or, in other words, a standard of conduct. The existence of a standard of conduct in its turn makes the most improbable achievement possible, by augmenting the power of endurance and of self-sacrifice amongst men who look to the past for their lessons and for their inspiration.

The story of the achievement of the Dover Patrol is merged in the greater proud record of the navy's protective part played with simplicity and self-sacrifice in the Great War of the twentieth century; yet that story has its own features, its own particular atmosphere, and its own importance.

The opening years of the nineteenth century had their Great War, too. Longer in its duration, it was carried on with less animosity. It was less in the nature of a struggle for dear life, and, except in its spirit, it was less intensely national. It did not involve in its toils the whole population. The issues at stake were as great, perhaps, but did not appear in such definite shapes to the great mass of the people which suffered its hardships and gave up its sons to its struggles. In its most obvious aspect that war, like the one of our day, was waged against an attempt at universal dominion. But it must be admitted that it was

also a war against the revolt of new-born ideas represented by a great and dominant figure issued from a
revolution and taking its own fatally conquering way
amongst the imperfectly awakened nations of Europe.
It was a struggle of the old certitudes against a man
embodying the new force of subversive beliefs.   It ran
its course, as momentous, if less ruthless, than the deadly
struggle in which the Dover Patrol has played its
part.   When it ended it left the world as weary, indeed, as it is to-day, but much less unsettled in its
thoughts and emotions about the spiritual value of its
monstrous experience.   Men's ideas were simpler then,
their sentiments less complex.   Their desires and
hopes, as poignant perhaps, remained still obscure.
The instinctive reaction against all the cruel negations
a war imposes on humanity had a less resentful character; and men's judgment of the attained issue was less
embittered by the effort they had been called upon
to make.   Yet their personal feelings were much like
our own.

When the hour of peace struck in 1815 there must
have been on board the King's ships anchored in the
Downs, patrolling in the Channel, in the squadrons on
distant stations, and in others cruising off nearly every
port of northern Europe—there must have been the
feeling that there never would be such a war again; a
feeling of relief, mingled, no doubt, with a half-acknowl-
edged sense of regret for the occupation that was gone.
The great question arising at the end of every pro-
longed effort made by mankind—And now—what next?
asked without misgivings in the consciousness of an
accomplished duty—was not free from a certain un-
easiness as to the days that would follow in other and
unknown conditions.   For a whole generation had
grown from boyhood to maturity with no knowledge

of peace conditions, and unperturbed by moral doubts
of its warlike achievement.

Amongst the men of the Dover Patrol assembled to
see the unveiling of the memorial to their own unforgettable dead there will be also a feeling of regret for
those days that are past, regret of the strenuous life
with its earnest purpose, its continuity of risk, its sense
of professional efficiency, its community of desperate
toil; regret even of those moments of extreme bodily
fatigue associated with that feeling of spiritual exal-
tation which enabled them each in his station, from
the Admiral commanding to the youngest member of
a small drifter's crew, to defy the enmity of nature and
the hostility of men.

Nobody would dream of apportioning shares of importance in the great task of the navy, so varied in its
unity, so diverse in its singleness of aim and its invariable purpose. But it is a fact that amongst all
those activities directed to the same end, exposed to
the same risk, making the same appeal, and entered
upon with the same courage, the work of the Dover
Patrol was very special work. The Dover Patrol held
the southern exit of the North Sea in the same way in
which the Grand Fleet may be said to have held its
northern entrance; and the greatness of its responsibility may be appreciated from the one dominant fact:
that on that Patrol rested the safety of our communica-
tions with the army in France, and that one of its
achievements was the safe passage across the Channel of
about seven million men without a single instance of
failure, in the presence of a superior enemy established
in force within easy striking distance on the flank of the
line; an enemy superior in numbers and material, holding
in his hands every element of successful attack except
for just a portion, an ever so small portion, of that sea

spirit animating the officers and men of the Dover command who stood in his way—including the very workers on shore in repair workshops and fitting-out sheds.

There was never a greater accord of fearless executive energy and skilled hard work than in the Dover Patrol. From the point of view of its spiritual harmony it was worthy to hold the extreme right wing of the great sea defence. Of its material success we all know by now; we have all heard of the millions of men transported to and fro across the Straits, of miles of nets laid along the coasts and kept in repair in defiance of heavy seas and long-range batteries, of mines swept along routes equalling in length twelve times the circumference of the globe, of merchant fleets of a hundred ships and more shepherded every day through the Downs. The eloquence of arithmetical figures as applied to the merits of the Dover Patrol is overwhelming indeed; but no figure of rhetoric can render justice to the quiet resolution of the men making up for the inadequacy of the means, the unavoidable inadequacy of the means for which only the force of circumstances was responsible, for which no past government can be blamed, since no one could have guessed the enormous scale of material requirements.

The means were inadequate, woefully inadequate; and thus the only trumps the Admiral of the Dover Patrol held in his hand at every turn of the dreadful game were the physical endurance, the inborn seamanship, the matter-of-fact, industrious, indefatigable enthusiasm with which every one under his orders threw his very soul into his appointed task. Threw it in and kept it there. It was no momentary effort. For the anxious days of the Dover Patrol were to be many, its nights full of dangers, its problems exacting, its duty calls incessant, and its men after all but the flesh and

blood of our common humanity. Their souls were the
only trumps in the desperate game, as he who was in
command must have felt at every moment of night and
day. It was a great and successful game, but it must
be confessed that for more than half the time it was a
game of bluff. It came off at every deal, England's
usual luck, that this time, too, has not failed her at the
hour of need! And England may well be proud of her
traditional luck in the character of her children serving
her at sea, on shore, and in the air.

The activities of the Dover Patrol were of many
kinds, but there were three imperative duties to which
all its energies had to be devoted: the safety of the
troop-transport service, the protection of merchant
shipping, the closing of the Channel exit against the
German submarines. One need not insist on their
vital importance for the army and the nation or on
the deadly danger of even a temporary failure. The
work had to be carried out with the slenderest conceiv-
able means, with obsolete torpedo destroyers, and with
unarmed drifters, in the presence of an enemy of superior force and possessing an infinite advantage in his
power to choose his own time for an attack of the most
deadly kind. Those three purely naval problems required incessant hard work, incessant risk, and incessant
vigilance. The routine of the Dover Patrol included
the boarding of ships, the regulation of traffic along the
cleared war lane, the laying of net and mine barrages
on the Belgian coast and across the Channel, their
guard and maintenance in all weathers and in all circumstances, with always present in all minds the sense
of numerical inferiority in a mission the failure of which
might have well brought about something not very far
from national disaster. In such conditions the stress

put upon the fortitude of every individual was bound to be very great.

The Dover Patrol was equal to it. Its devotion, expressed in a plodding, dogged perseverance, stood the test of frequent severe losses in men and ships, and of continuous severe strain on its mental and physical faculties as a whole. The tale of the Dover Patrol is the tale of a small nucleus of ships and crews of the Royal Navy, and round it of a great number of other men and other vessels, mostly fisher-folk and fisher-craft, with the addition of Merchant Service men and of R.N.R. and R.N.V.R. officers and ratings. Though, properly speaking, not belonging to the fighting service, all those men lived up to their old tradition and were found sufficient for the trust reposed in them.

They were found sufficient. No praise could be more adequately expressed, when one looks at the magnitude of the trust and the arduous character of the operations it imposed upon the men and the ships of the Dover command. Originating in the simple Downs Boarding Flotilla, under the orders of the naval officer commanding at Harwich, the Dover Patrol developed an independent existence and by the establishment of fortified German naval bases on the coast of Flanders acquired an importance in the scheme of naval defence which cannot well be exaggerated. The reinforcements and supplies for the army, the food for the country, demanded the safety of the Straits. Had the enemy probed the weakness of the Dover Patrol and broken with his overwhelming force through that thin defence to invade the waters of the Channel, it would have been a disaster, the fatal consequences of which imagination even now shrinks from contemplating.

The great sailor-like qualities of the Dover Patrol,

the consummate seamanship displayed in the planning
and execution of its incessant operations, its steady
manner of meeting deadly emergencies, its cool vigilance
in the presence of an ever-menacing situation, may well
compel the admiration of any man who knows something, however little, of the demands of sea service.
To the risks of actual warfare the crews of the drifters
watching over the barrage nets were often helplessly
exposed. But nothing could dismay either the naval
or the auxiliary branches of the Dover Patrol. These
men were concerned about the perfection of their work,
but the sudden flash of German guns in the night
troubled them not at all. As, indeed, why should it?
In their early days some of them had but a single rifle
on board to meet the three four-inch guns of German
destroyers. Unable to put up a fight and without speed
to get away, they made a sacrifice of their lives every
time they went out for a turn of duty; they concen-
trated their valour on the calm, seamanlike execution
of their work amongst the exploding mines and bursting
shells. It was their conception of their honour, and
they carried it out of this war unblemished by a single
display of weakness, by the slightest moment of hesitation in the long tale of dangerous service.

In this simple way these seamen, professional and un-
professional, naval and civilian, have earned for themselves the memorial erected to their faithful labours.
The record of the Dover Patrol's work contains a great
moral and a good many professional lessons for their
children and their successors; the incalculable value of
a steady front, the perfecting of nets, the exact process
of laying barrages in a tideway, the evolving of an in-
genious method for night bombardments, and of a
system of long-range firing—a whole great store of new
ideas and new practice laid up for future use. But in

truth that which in the last instance kept the German forces from breaking disastrously on any dark night into the Channel, and jeopardizing the very foundations of our resisting power, was not the wonderfully planned and executed defences of nets and mines, but the indomitable hearts of the men of the Dover Patrol.

MEMORANDUM

On the Scheme for Fitting Out a Sailing Ship for the Purpose of Perfecting the Training of Merchant Service Officers Belonging to the Port of Liverpool

Assuming that the generous public spirit of the Liverpool shipowners will find the capital necessary for the building and equipping a southern-going sailing ship to perfect the training of the officers of the Mercantile Marine, I conceive that the cost of running such a ship—that is: wages, upkeep, repairs, general surveys and insurance—ought to be covered by what she may earn as a cargo carrier on the training voyages which will be planned for her.

Here I will submit to the originators of the scheme that a voyage to an Australian port (including New Zealand) out by the Cape and round by the Horn would be the best for such a purpose. My reasons are: the healthy climate of that part of the world, the number of the meteorological regions traversed which will develop sound judgment as to weather, the comparative facility of the voyage, combined with a great variety of general experience which a round trip of that sort will offer. The length of passages need not be an objection; the complete training of a young seaman ought to include the experience of many days together at sea between water and sky. It would have a spiritual and practical value for him even if he is destined never to be out of sight of land for more than a few days in his future professional life.

I

Assuming then that the ship would be expected to be self-supporting (and no more) it is my deliberate opinion that her size should be limited strictly to the tonnage which will enable her under modern conditions to pay her expenses. I venture to suggest (however shocking it may appear to the minds of men who own and manage fleets of large steamships) fourteen to fifteen hundred tons, or as near thereto as is consistent with the earning of her expenses, as the proper tonnage for the ship. I admit that I don't know what the best freight-carrying capacity of a ship is at the present time; but I beg the Committee charged with the elaboration of the scheme to allow me to expose my reasons for what I advance in support of the above opinion. I must premise here that in all that I am going to say I will be drawing on my own experience as a seaman trained to his duties under the British flag and, in regard to the performance of such duties, having a good record for more than sixteen years of sea life, both in sail and steam.

My contention is that for sea-going qualities, ease of handling, quickness in manœuvring, and even in point of actual safety, if caught in a bad position, nothing can beat a, say, 1400-ton ship, designed so as to have a dead weight carrying capacity of about once and a half her registered tonnage. The same remark may be applied to the comfort in bad weather when, it must be remembered, the men managing her propelling machinery must remain exposed on the deck instead of being sheltered under it. The latest big sailing ship (in so far as she still exists) is generally in that respect what the sailors graphically describe as a mere "bathing-machine," her enormous main deck, especially when running before a heavy sea, being always full of water and extremely uncomfortable, besides being dangerous for that very reason. Also, the great length necessarily given to those big ships of three thousand tons and over makes them clumsy to handle, anything but quick in manœuvre, and renders them rather helpless, from their very size, in case of any serious damage either aloft or about the rudder. It is also to be remarked that a ship's quick response in manœuvring develops a corresponding activity and smartness in her crew.

I beg the gentlemen concerned with this scheme to understand that I am not speaking as a literary person indulging his fancy but as the usual sort of Merchant Service officer who has served in all sorts of ships and draws upon his ordinary experience; with this advantage, only, that he had time to think about it and meditate over its lessons. Pursuing the matter further, I wish also to touch on the question of the ship's appearance. In a steamship the increase of size certainly makes for good looks, adding to the inherent beauty of the lines an expression of power and dignity which arouses one's admiration. It is not so with a sailing vessel. Hardly any ship of over 2000 tons I have ever seen escaped giving an impression which may be best defined by the word "overgrown"; and I have a good many in my memory to whom nothing but the sailors' graphic phrase "a big, clumsy brute" could in justice be applied. Now, in view of the end which the Liverpool shipowners have in equipping a sailing ship, that is to *perfect* the training of officers for their fleets, certain ideal elements must be taken into consideration. It is very necessary that those boys should grow attached to their ship (an easy thing for a sailor to do), be proud of her individual appearance, of her sea qualities, of their association with her; and that they should remember their period of training, not as a horrible grind in discomfort and without personal gratification of any kind, but as a great time in their lives; an experience it has been their privilege as seamen of the Port of Liverpool to go through; a time to be remembered with pleasure and pride, somewhat as an old public-school boy looks back at his old school, the beauty of its old buildings and the prestige of its traditions. The greatest achievements of Merchant Service seamen have been performed in ships of between 900 to 1600 tons, in the way of record passages (which were then the exclusive merit of seamen), of feats in clever handling and in the bringing in of disabled ships to port by their own seamanship and determination without any outside assistance. And if the objection is made that I am advocating things hopelessly out of date, then my answer will be that in this scheme of *perfected* training associated so closely with men's *morale* and with old traditions, the out-of-dateness argument does not apply. On the practical side that objection may be met by pointing out that those boys are not to be trained for officers of modern sailing ships, but to be *perfected* as future officers of the finest modern steamships. Therefore, what is important is to give them for their training not the most modern sailing ship (which in any case is doomed and need not be taken into consideration at all), but to select for them the *best* period of sailing-ship practice and service.

One more consideration I want to present to the originators of the scheme, which is this: that in a very large sailing ship there is always a tendency to supply her (on account of the difficulty of manning her effectively) with a lot of labour-saving appliances. This brings me to the second postulate which, after the size of the ship, I am most anxious to submit for consideration. And it is this:

II

That there should be no labour-saving appliances in the shape of steam winches and so on; and that the hoisting of the sails, the working of the boats, and the general physical work of the sailor's calling should be done by man power, of which, of course, the cadets on board would be the principal part. A vertical boiler, mainly for the purpose of heaving up the anchors, may be advisable; but the windlass should be of the kind which can be also worked by the crew by means of a capstan on the forecastle-head.

My reasons for this insistence on the use of man power are as follows: First of all, there is no necessity for anything else. With forty boys out of any given batch on board (Mr. Holt mentions eighty as the number and on that point I will offer a remark later) of an advanced physical development and certain weight of body, together with a ship's crew of, say, twelve A. B.'s, four petty officers, and some other ratings, the officers ought to be able to handle a ship, of the size and rig I am thinking of, like a plaything. Secondly, it may be laid down as an axiom that no labour done on board ship in the way of duty is either too hard or in any way unworthy of the best effort and attention or, so to speak, beneath the dignity of any youngster wishing to fit himself to be a good officer. Thirdly, there is undoubtedly something elevating in physical work into which one puts all one's heart in association with others and for a clearly understood purpose. Apart from that it will bring these youths into a more intimate contact with the propelling machinery of the ship and they will, so to speak, learn the feel of it. It mustn't be forgotten that seamen's work was never looked upon or had the character of mere slavish toil, as some branches of labour on shore tend to become. In its essence life at sea has been always a healthy life, and part of that was owing to the very nature of the physical exertions required. I affirm with profound conviction that sailing-ship life is an excellent physical developer. I have repeatedly seen a delicate youngster brought on board by an anxious relative change out of all knowledge into a stout youth during a twelvemonth's voyage. I have never seen an apparently delicate boy break down under the conditions of the sea life of my time. They *all* improved. Moreover, any physical work intelligently done develops a special mentality; in this case it would be the sailor mentality; surely a valuable acquisition for a sea officer either in sail or steam.

III

The sailing ship, then, I have in my eye (something very much like the Liverpool *Sierras* which were afloat between '80 and '90) would be a hull of between 1400 and 1500 tons register with a dead weight capacity of over 2000 tons, in which case it would be sufficient for her to have three square-rigged masts. If the tonnage of the ship is raised to 2000 tons register then there must be four masts, of which the aftermost one would be rigged fore and aft. In any case, I would advocate for the training ship a long poop and a very roomy forecastle head; the poop, if the vessel is three-masted, extending as far as the main rigging; and the object being to reduce the area of the main deck as much as possible. This would tend to make the ship much more comfortable. Ships with long poops are always the driest in all weathers and safest for the individuals having to move about the decks in heavy weather. The main deck would have on it a deck house in the space between the fore coaming of the main hatch and the foremast; leaving a clear passage across at each end and having wide alleyways on each side. The house would contain the vertical boiler for raising steam for the windlass; the accommodation for the ship's crew and the berths of the ship's petty officers. Under the forecastle head there would be space at the sides for various storerooms, or the electric light plant, if carried, could be installed on one side and the storerooms on the other. All that, however, may be left to the skill and ingenuity of the designer, once the actual size of the ship and the number of people she has to carry, all told, has been decided upon.

In this matter I have a certain competence because I was for 2 years chief officer of a sailing passenger ship running between London and Adelaide and I believe the very last of her kind, with the exception perhaps of the *Macquarrie* (later training ship for New Zealand merchant cadets), where the experience of a comparatively large number of persons on board ship could be obtained by the sailing-ship officer. She was only 1270 tons register and the greatest number of people I had on board of her was 113 all told. She had room for 50 passengers when full and we had perforce to carry a lot of live stock, a milk cow for the children and so on; yet her space was not inconveniently crowded, and no passenger ever complained of cramped accommodation, and generally they made the round trip in her. She carried outwards a general cargo and in Adelaide loaded the usual Australian cargo, for the most part wool. Her poop was 78 feet long over all; under that we carried eleven double passenger cabins on each side, two cabins for the mates, a large pantry amidships and a doctor's berth and surgery. The accommodation for the captain consisted of two stern cabins, both very roomy, of which one was his stateroom and the other was planned and furnished as a sitting room, which he never used at sea, sharing the saloon with the passengers. This saloon contained two long tables at which all the people berthed under the poop deck could sit down to meals. I think that this arrangement could be adopted with advantage in the cadet ship under contemplation. The artificial lighting of the *Torrens* being oil and candles required extreme vigilance, but assuming the Liverpool cadets berthed in cabins as above, if electric light is to be introduced the lamps could be set in the partitions between them, so that each lamp would light two cabins. The long saloon would be the common room for navigational studies and meals, the electric lighting of that space, however economically applied, would be always better than the lamp-lighting of that ship which was sufficient for the passengers to read, write, or play their games in the evening. There were never any complaints on that score. The captain of a training ship would probably use all his accommodation at sea too, messing by himself. Apart from that it seems to me that the man entrusted with the responsible position of commanding such a training ship would wish to keep in as close touch with the boys as conformable with the preservation of proper merchant-ship discipline; and that he would not find the nearness of his cabin to the bulk of them either inconvenient or irksome.

The accommodation on the poop, being sufficient only for about 44 cadets, could be duplicated to a certain extent below, aft, on the twin deck, and be made accessible by means of the after hatch, fitted with a proper companionway. There may be some difficulty with the supply of daylight down there and in that respect the berths below would be inferior, but as there would be no doubt different grades among the boys in the way of seniority and ratings, a boy would be moved by seniority or on promotion from below to above at some time or other in the course of his training. This would be something to look forward to; and in this connection I would remark that the comfort of the boys should be cared for strictly within the limits of due regard for their health, physical development and opportunity for study, and no more. The greatest simplicity in such arrangements compatible with health and self-respect should be the note; and I believe that no boy properly constituted and wishing to be a seaman will resent such a system.

I suppose that as regards the boys, at least, a three-watch system will be introduced; though I must confess that I have never seen a boy hurt by the watch and watch duty which in my time all of them had to go through during the four years of their apprenticeship. In that case, however, the utmost vigilance and alertness in the time of duty should be exacted by the officer of the watch from the cadets at their various stations, whether at the lee helm with the helmsman, or on the lookout with an A. B. of the ship's crew, or about the decks at the different sheets, tacks and braces they may be specially told off to. The disadvantage of the three-watch system is that the cadet will be always on duty at the same hours. Some system of shifts should be introduced if only to change the boys in rotation from one watch to another; for the habit of wakefulness is also a matter of training, and the boys should be accustomed to keep their alertness at all periods of the night. I would suggest that the senior cadets (especially those who had obtained the rating of cadet petty officer) should be employed as assistants to the officer of the watch to the fullest possible extent; and when sufficiently advanced be entrusted with the trimming of the yards, the taking in or setting of light sails in manageable weather, and so on. The progression of stations will be, I imagine, from waist-cadets to mizzen-topmen, through main and fore to forecastlemen, which last would be selected from the strongest and the most advanced, during the training course of eighteen months. I imagine that the training ship with some luck in her weather and with quick dispatch at either end, could do two round voyages in that time. The *Torrens*, a fast ship, could have done it with ease, though as a matter of fact she made one voyage every eleven months, but then she would lie for weeks on the berth, both in London and Port Adelaide.

That ship carried four anchors, that is, three bowers and one stream, besides one big and one small kedge, and this is the number that would be sufficient for the training ship. Of course, the anchors would be stock anchors. In this connection I wish to remark that if the anchor is hove up by steam the catting and fishing should be done by hand under all circumstances with the help of the forecastle-head capstan. As to the sails, I assume that she would carry (unless she is to be really a very big ship) six topsails, three topgallantsails, three royals, four or three headsails, the usual number of staysails; and, I suggest, two courses. The crossjack course may be done away with. In my first year on board the *Torrens* we abolished that sail mainly out of regard for the feelings of the passengers who had their chairs placed all about the mizzenmast; and it made no difference whatever to the speed of the ship. The fair weather mizzen staysail, which was a particularly big sail, replaced it perfectly at all trims, from sharp up to two points abaft the beam. With the wind aft the crossjack was merely a nuisance.

I advocate the ship carrying single topgallantsails as a matter of traditional practice and training. For the same reason I would suggest that the clew lines of the upper sails and the clew-garnets of the courses should be led to the quarters of the yard and not to the yardarm. The proper furling of a sail, with a smooth bunt and tightly rolled yardarms, was a great point in the habits of smartness and proper merchant-ship discipline. It was also a matter of correct seamanship, because a sail that was not properly furled in bad weather was likely to free itself and blow away from the yard. The shifting of clew lines to the yardarms was really a dodge of undermanning, since it is obvious that with no bunt to the sail less men are required to make some sort of furl of it. The training ship, however, will be anything but undermanned, and unless she were very big there would be plenty of hands in her to furl the three topgallantsails together. I have repeatedly seen the four boys of the *Torrens* with the addition of one able seaman furl the main topgallantsail of that ship in a stiff breeze. In a ship of 1600 tons six boys and two able seamen ought to master a topgallantsail in almost any weather. When I joined the *Torrens* the then master of her, Captain Cope (an old Conway boy), fell in at once with my suggestion to shift the clew lines back to the quarters of the yard, on the ground that the ship was manned well enough to do things properly.

In regard to boats, I will again refer to my experience of the *Torrens* (a sailing ship with a hundred souls on board). We carried in her, aft, two quarter-boats on davits abreast the mizzen rigging. They were well above water, toggled-in against a spar so as to be disengaged by one single jerk on a lanyard (their tackle falls being always coiled clear on deck), and in other respects were ready for lowering instantly. Owing to the shortness of a merchantman's crew the orders as to these boats were that in an emergency the nearest men (up to four) were to get into her at once, the officer of the watch and the midshipman of the watch attending to the falls. The only real test of quickness we had happened in the daytime and in light weather, when the ship was luffed up till the sails lifted and one of the quarter-boats was lowered to pick up a parrot which had flown overboard. Not having been on deck at the time I don't know how long all this took, but the parrot survived the experience; so we must have been quick enough to have saved a child, for instance, of which we always had several on board.

On the skids abaft the mainmast we carried two bigger spare boats bottom up and not ready for lowering. But the principal boats of the ship were two very roomy lifeboats, carried on skids forward, just abaft the fore rigging. They stood in chocks and their davits were fore-and-afted at sea, but the lowering tackles were always hooked and the falls coiled in tubs secured on the top of the deck house, of which I have spoken before. Those lifeboats were fitted out ready to "abandon ship," with sea anchors, oil bags, oars, mast and sail, blue lights, water beakers and ship's bread in tins. Their chocks were held in position by a bolt in the usual way and the ship's carpenter was instructed when making his report to me in the morning to report: "Davits and bolts free." When the bolt was knocked out a lift of three inches was all that was necessary to swing out those lifeboats. Now and again

I had a test, generally at eight o'clock in the morning at the change of watches, and I managed to bring things to a point when the whole operation took seven minutes from the time of the order: "Both watches. Out lifeboats," to the moment when they were swung back and landed again in their chocks; the second mate taking charge of the starboard and the senior apprentice (acting third) of the port side. This for a merchant ship was quite as good as could be expected and would have met almost any emergency short of sudden disaster. In the Channel and between the chops of the Channel and the Western Islands (either homeward or outward bound), on the first appearance of thick weather with a moderate sea, it was a standing order that the officer of the watch immediately after calling the captain was to swing these boats outboard ready for lowering. In that position they remained, weather permitting, till the fog cleared.

I have entered into those details because from the nature of things there can be very few sailing-ship officers left now who have had the experience of the care of upwards of a hundred people on board a 1300-ton ship. How far the boys should be given an insight into the stowage of a large single hold I am not prepared to say. The proper stowage of a sailing ship was an extremely important part of her preparation for sea, affecting her sailing powers, the comfort of everybody on board, and even her absolute safety. The stowage of a subdivided hold of a large steamship is from the very nature of things a much less nice matter. It is also different in its nature, since the order of the ports of call is a paramount consideration in the disposition of a steamship's cargo. But an insight into the old conditions cannot do any harm and may be found useful on occasion.

Next I venture to offer the suggestion that the ship should have no auxiliary propulsion of any kind. Let her *be* a sailing ship. I don't exactly know how this may affect the rate of insurance, but I assure you that a very few years ago, well within the life of the man who is addressing you now, nobody thought a sailing ship less safe than a steamship. A ship's safety, apart from the "Act of God," rests in the hands of the men who are aboard of her, from the highest to the lowest in their different degrees. Machinery, *per se*, will not make a ship more safe, and the saved space would be useful for other purposes.

The ship will have, of course, to make use of tugs at the end of her passages. This will afford the cadets an opportunity to get an insight into the various points of seamanship connected with the operations of towage. The mere handling of steel and other kinds of hawsers will by itself give them valuable practice.

General Remarks: Finally I beg leave to touch upon the actual number of people on board. Mr. Laurence Holt's letter speaks of 60 to 80 cadets. I should suggest that the lesser number should be adopted. And even less than 60 if possible. What I have in my mind is the possibility of some accident (which may happen to the best ship afloat) and its effect on the public mind. Regard ought to be paid also to the facility of getting a lesser number of people out of a sinking ship or saving them all in case of a shipwreck.

I have assumed that the period of training would be eighteen months. This in the case of a Conway boy would work out his apprenticeship as follows: One year sea service allowed for Conway training; one year and a half in the sailing ship; the last year and a half as apprentice or cadet in a steamship.

In case of boys joining straight from a school on

shore I suppose they would be kept for two and a half years on board the sailing vessel and finish their time in steam.

I don't touch on the point of navigational studies, for which no doubt a provision will be made. I will only remark that the greatest care and accuracy should be required from the cadets acting as assistant officers of the watch (and generally from all senior boys) in keeping the ship's dead reckoning. This is a point of seamanship rather than navigation.

The ship, whether at anchor or alongside the quay, ought to offer that aspect of finished smartness alow and aloft that a training ship should have. It must be remembered that wherever she goes she will be representing the entire maritime community of the Port of Liverpool, employers and employed, shipowners and seamen.

The cadets going ashore on leave should always wear the ship's uniform, unless specifically invited to play games. The ship will no doubt have a football team and a cricket eleven.

A harbour watch (as distinguished from anchor watch), composed of one senior and two junior cadets, should be kept. And, generally, a proper amount of formality should be observed in the ship's routine both at sea and in port. It is conducive to self-respect in all ranks.

THE LOSS OF THE *DALGONAR*

To the Editor of the London *Mercury*

Sir,

Since you have invited comments from nautical readers on a certain obscure passage in the "True Story" printed in your September number, I will refer here to the point raised by Mr. L. C. Gane and to some other mistakes of minor importance. Not that I think they matter in the least for your readers, who, in any case, would have perceived the great quality of the narrative.

The passage queried by Mr. L. C. Gane, quite justifiably, runs as follows:

"At noon wore ship . . . 7 P. M. wind and sea increasing, took in the *mizzen fore upper topsail.* 11 P. M. wind and sea still increasing, took in the *mizzen and main upper topsails.*"

The italicized words have, nautically speaking, no sense; the first four absolutely, the second five in relation to the first statement; since it is obvious that the mizzen upper topsail could not have been taken in twice.

These are obviously slips of the pen or errors of transcription. The first statement evidently was meant for: "Took in the mizzen and fore upper topsails," the word missing in your text being the "and" after the word "mizzen." The ship then was carrying her fore-sail, lower fore-topsail, lower and upper main-topsail and lower mizzen-topsail. At 11 P. M., the gale still increasing, the sails taken in were the "mizzen *lower*

81

and main upper topsails," the word missing in the phrase as it stands in the text being the word "lower" after the word "mizzen." Thus, at 11 P. M. the ship was reduced down to her foresail and the fore and main lower topsails, which was a possible and seamanlike canvas for her to carry in the then state of the weather. I cannot, however, defend myself from the impression conveyed by the narrative and also from what happened afterwards, that the foresail was carried on her too long. That large piece of canvas must have had the effect (at least at times) of forcing the ship one and a half or perhaps two knots through the water—for no object that I can see. And *there* was the danger. But it is easy to be wise after the event!

The paragraph queried by Mr. Gane contains also a printing error: the plural "s" should come out of the word "foresails." A ship has got only one foresail.

As to other minor corrections, the words *"main draft"* in the opening paragraph of the story should be *"mean draft,"* as is obvious from the inspection of the figures. The draught of water is a formal logbook entry in any ship about to proceed to sea. Another misprint (on page 483) consists in a superfluous letter. The line runs: "and *web* squared-in the main and crossjack yards, etc., etc." The "b" got in there by mistake. It should, of course, run: "and *we* squared-in the main, etc.," in what is a correct description of wearing ship, which was the last manœuvre attempted before the *Dalgonar* became unmanageable.

On the next page the meaningless word printed as "nil" should, of course, be "rail."

I agree with all my heart with the editorial note heading the story. There can be nothing finer or more simple. The crew of the *Dalgonar* behaved as well as I have ever seen the crew of a British merchant ship behave in a critical situation, and they deserve fully the encomiums and blessings Mr. Mull, the Chief Officer, gives to them in his report written on board the *Loire*. A tribute of admiration is due, too, to the captain of the French ship for his humane determination to save those men, and for the display of seaman-like resolution and skill in maintaining his ship in position for so long in such desperate weather. Nobody but a seaman can appreciate the risks and the difficulty of the task, and the severe strain put on the endurance of the crew and officers of the *Loire* in sheer physical exertions, in unremitting vigilance and plucky seamanship, which enabled them to remain by and finally to take off the crew of the *Dalgonar*.

Yours, etc.,

JOSEPH CONRAD.

TRAVEL

A Preface to Richard Curle's "Into the East"

There is no fate so uncertain as the fate of books of travel. They are the most assailable of all men's literary productions. The man who writes a travel book delivers himself more than any other into the hands of his enemies. The popularizing scientific writer's position is much more secure. His very subject is, properly speaking, marvellous in itself, and for that reason the intelligent multitude swallows it eagerly, or at least receives it with open mouth, and forms its own amazing conclusions. A writer of fiction —well!—he romances all the time, and the truth he has in him being disguised in various garments, from gold mantles to rags, is almost beyond the reach of criticism. All really he has got to attend to is grammar and punctuation. Metaphysics, of course, are simply intoxicating for those who like that way of killing our appointed time in this valley of tears. But as to those whose fancy leads them to investigate more or less profoundly that same valley. . . !

But after all a traveller is very much to be envied. He is to be envied for the instinct that prompts him, for the courage that sustains him. He is to be admired for enduring a spectacle almost intolerably gorgeous and varied, but with only hints, here and there, of dramatic scenes, with, practically, no star actors in it, with the knowledge that the curtain will not fall for months and months to come; and that he must play the

exacting part of a spectator of those human characteristics and activities, in their picturesque, ugly, or savage
settings, without, so to speak, the prospect of going
home to bed presently. Imagine a lover of drama and
of stage effects forced to sleep in his very stall, and every
day, opening his eyes upon a never-ceasing performance. The taste for that sort of thing may well be
envied as evidence of capacity for mental and physical
resistance, not only against the strain of all the "things
that seem to be," but against one's own weakness.
Perhaps that is the reason why the Arabs, racially
great travellers and great lovers of wonders, invented
the proverb, "Travelling is victory," which stands
as the motto of this book. It expresses, indeed, a
romantic conception. But there is a soberness of
temperament in the Arab race which has prevented it
from rushing exultingly into the writing of travel
books. Of course, I am an ignorant person, from
circumstances which it would not be to my advantage
to disclose, but I can only call to mind one Arab
traveller who has written a book; and surely if there
had been shoals of them I would have heard of another.

Those people did much of their travelling sword in
hand and with the name of the One God on their lips.
But theirs were personally conducted parties, as
destructive to the peace and the spiritual character of
places they visited as any crowd from a tourist agency
invading the shades of Vallombrosa. Let us forget the
Arabs as well as their successors who are achieving
victory every year at the price of so many pounds per
head for a certain number of days. They demand
neither our admiration nor our pity.

Nowadays many people encompass the globe. That
kind of victory became to a certain extent fashionable
for some years after the piercing of the Isthmus of

Suez. Multitudes rushed through that short cut with blank minds and, alas, also blank notebooks where the megalomania, from which we all more or less suffer, got recorded in the shape of "Impressions." The inanity of the mass of travel books the Suez Canal is responsible for took the proportions of an enormous and melancholy joke. For it was a mournful sight to see so many people giving themselves away. Their books covered private shelves and the tables of *cabinets de lecture* in a swarm more devastating to the world's freshness of impression than a swarm of locusts in a field of young corn. When that visitation began I was quite a boy and in my innocence I read them all, or, at least, all I could lay my hands on. Women, single or in pairs, fashionable couples, professors of intense gravity, facetious business men—I read all their travel books, including even Baron Hübner's "Voyage Round the World," which, I should think, remains unequalled to this day.

That category of travellers with their parrot-like remarks, their strange attempts at being funny, and their lamentable essays in seriousness has apparently passed away. Or perhaps they only print their books for circulation amongst friends. I suspect, however, they have ceased to write simply because there are too many of them. They do not appear as travellers even to the most naïve minds and perhaps even to their own minds. They are simply an enormous company of people who go round the world for a change and rest, either suffering from overwork (whatever that may mean) or from neurasthenia. And I am sure my best wishes go with them for an easy and radical recovery. Steamship companies love them.

Sporting travellers form a class by themselves. They mostly write for other sportsmen, though I must confess that their books hold for me even now some fascination. They are apt to grow monotonous in the descriptive statistics of slaughter and as to the shortcomings of their "boys." Also in their admiration for their trackers, who seem all to have been made from the same pattern. I have noticed them adopting of late years a half-apologetic tone about their exploits; whereas the men of twenty-five years ago, with their much less perfect weapons and their big records, were frankly exulting. Frankness is a virtue I like. I would respect the modern attitude more if I were sure of its absolute genuineness. Moderation in game killing is enforced now by many regulations; but on considering how easy it is not to shoot an antelope one becomes slightly doubtful of the perfect candour of men who travel thousands of miles in dreary steamboats and uncomfortable primitive trains for sport. On the other hand, I admit that a sportsman who would consistently miss every antelope would be an extremely uninteresting person. The world of explorers and discoverers, the heroes of my boyhood, has vanished almost to nothing in the nineteenth century. Some of them wrote the classics of travel, but no passage of years can dim my admiration for their selfless spirit and manly faithfulness to their task pursued in solitude or with a few devoted henchmen, persevered in through numberless days with death only a pace behind, but with a calm mind and a steady heart.

What about mere wanderers?—those individuals that one meets in various fairly well-known localities, but who come upon one round unexpected corners, often shabby and depressed, sometimes haggard and jaunty; with tales in their mouths of the flattest description or of a comic quality bordering on tears; with, now and then, a story that would frighten you to death if you were one of those men who don't know how to smile in time. I would class them as an outcast tribe if it did not sound so rude. And I would not be rude for anything to people capable of starting on their travels with their hands, and very little else besides, in their pockets. I have known amongst them men of ruffianly mental complexion, cultivating a truculent manner and a cold steady stare, who, if it were possible to bluff one's own destiny, might have been sitting in high places. And I ask myself, in my half-reluctant partiality for the class, whether some of them have not achieved it. But success disguises them at once and contemporary history gives them other names.

In my review of the categories of men who move about the earth I come now to the real travellers who wrote books, the protagonists of the modern travellers, in the same way, I may say, in which Hannon may be looked upon as a protagonist of the discoverers and the circumnavigators of the globe. Only the *Periplus* was probably a dreary official report. At any rate it has not come down to us. The outstanding figure amongst those men who dedicated their books of travel to popes and emperors is Marco Polo, with his meticulous descriptive gift, his cautious credulity, his eye for splendour and his historian's rather than a traveller's temperament. He gave his readers what the readers of that day wanted, historical facts in a foreign and gorgeous atmosphere. But the time for such books of travel is past on this earth girt about with cables, with an atmosphere made restless by the waves of ether, lighted by that sun of the twentieth century under which there is nothing new left now, and but very little of what may still be called obscure.

The day of many-volumed "Journeys, through or to," of "Relations of this or that" (and much charm and

ability some of them had), the days of heroic travel are
gone; unless, of course, in the newspaper sense, in which
heroism like everything else in the world becomes as
common if not as nourishing as our daily bread. There
would be always a lady or a gentleman ready to discover with considerable fuss a bit of territory of, say,
ten square miles, resembling exactly the surrounding
and already explored lands; or interview some new
ruler, like a reflection in a dim and tarnished mirror of
some real chieftain in the books of a hundred years
ago; or marvel at a disagreeable fish of ferocious habits
which had been described already in some old-time,
simply worded, unsensational "Relation." But even
this is a game which is losing its interest, and in a very
little time will have come to an end. Presently there
will be no backyard left in the heart of Central Africa
that has not been peeped into by some person more or
less commissioned for the purpose. The Nigeria of
Barth, of Denham, of Clapperton, of Mungo Park, of
other infinitely curious and profoundly inspired men,
will be bristling with police posts, colleges, tramway
poles, and all those improving things triumphantly
recorded, and always with the romantic addition that,
within twenty miles, the hills, or the forests, or the
holes in the sand, or the depths of the jungle (that
blessed word) are swarming with cannibal tribes
miraculously restrained by one white man with two
black soldiers and his native cook for all company.
And the great cloud of fatuous daily photographs and
even more fatuous descriptive chatter, under whose
shadow no traveller could live, will brood over those
seldom-visited places of the world that, despoiled of
their old black soul of mystery, have not yet acquired
its substitute, which will be marvellously piebald when
it comes.

This moment of ill-humour with "things as they are becoming" is of course perfectly unreasonable and even perverse, which is worse. It would not deserve to be tolerated except for its inherent piety. As a matter of fact I have been thinking for a moment of the dead, of the great and good travellers loved in my boyhood, as I laid aside the MS. of this modern traveller who by publishing it has delivered himself to his enemies. He is very modern, for he is fashioned by the conditions of an explored earth in which the latitudes and longitudes having been recorded once for all have become things of no importance, in the sense that they can no longer appeal to the spirit of adventure, inflame no imagination, lead no one up to the very gates of mortal danger.

These basic facts of geography having been ascertained by the observations of heavenly bodies, the glance of the modern traveller contemplating the much-surveyed earth beholds in fact a world in a state of transition; very different in this from the writers of travel books of Marco Polo's time, who in their conscientious narratives seem to progress amongst immutable wonders, to feed their curiosity on a consistency of the splendid and the bizarre, presented to their eyes to stare at, to their minds to moralize upon.

And those things, which stand as if imperishable in the pages of old books of travel, are all blown away, have vanished as utterly as the smoke of the travellers' camp fires in the icy night air of the Gobi Desert, as the smell of incense burned in the temples of strange gods, as the voices of Asiatic statesmen speculating with the cruel wisdom of past ages on matters of peace and war.

Nothing obviously strange remains for our eyes now. The Khan of Tartary's court ceremonies were certainly marvellous in quite a different sense from the procedure

followed at Kuala Kangsar two years ago, when the
Sultan of Perak was invested with the K. C. M. G.
by the Governor of the Straits Settlements. This
modern traveller describes it all in less words than
Marco Polo would have used paragraphs on such a
striking occasion. It was curious for him to watch
under the formal routine of official compliments the
Malay princes play up to British etiquette, while graft-
ing it on their own ideas of politeness, and wearing, he
thought, a slightly ironical smile on their dark faces.
And to think that only fifty years ago, after a certain
amount of jungle and stockade fighting, the Sultan
of Perak, or perhaps his brother ruler next door in
Selangor, having listened attentively to a lecture from
a British Admiral on the heinousness of a certain
notable case of piracy, turned round quickly to his
attending chiefs and to the silent throng of his Malay
subjects, exclaiming, "Hear now, my people! Don't
let us have any more of this little game." Those words
ought to have been engraved in letters of gold on a
marble monument at the mouth of the Jugra River;
for from the moment they were pronounced dates the
era of security for the poor folks of the coast, for the
fishermen and traders in the Straits of Malacca. The
downfall of local piracy in fact. The world in transition!

Our very curiosities have changed, growing more
subtle amongst the vanishing mysteries of the earth.
Very appropriately this modern traveller reclining
on the verandah of the State Rest-house, after having
watched the ceremonies of installation in the blaring
of trumpets and the gorgeous bright colours of the
throng, recalls the strong impression of, one might say,
indifferent and rather contemptuous good-will between
brown and white, and gives himself up to the vain (as
he himself observes) occupation of speculating on the

future of countries. But he does it not in the spirit of a statesman looking for political truth, but in the doubting mood of a traveller of our day who on the very threshold of the East has questioned himself as to the ultimate truth of travel; whether perchance it was no more than the mastery of first impressions; and whether the sanity of our outlook on the world consists in secret revolt against its facts but in the final acceptance of the whole, or in the conformity with all the multiple forms and the mental rejection of life's inscrutable purpose? It is this mood which makes him so responsive to the inner promptings suggested by travel, which informs the felicitous rendering of his visual impressions. This it is that forces him, while looking out into the night from the deck of an Irrawaddy flotilla steamer, to admit to himself man's secret antagonism to the wilderness; or during his few hours' stay in Bhamo, a town on the very frontier of the Chinese enigma, where caravans incessantly come and go through mysterious valleys and where people live on rumours from day to day, to absorb its spirit of secrecy and waiting and hear suddenly around him "the whisper of innumerable hills passing on one to another the restless murmur of men's hearts." Very modern in impressions, in appreciations, in curiosities, and in his very love of the mother earth, of whose children he has written subtly and tenderly in some three volumes of characteristic tales; a traveller of our day, condemned to make his discoveries on beaten tracks, he looks on, sensitive, meditative, with delicate perceptions and a gift for expression, alive to the saving grace of human and historical associations; and while pursuing amongst the men busy with ascertained facts the riddles presented by a world in transition, he seems to have captured for us the spirit of modern travel itself.

STEPHEN CRANE

On a rainy day of March of the year 1923, listening to the author of this biography telling me of his earnest labours for the memory of a man who was certainly unique in his generation, I exclaimed to myself with wonder: "And so it has come to pass after all—this thing which I did not expect to see!" In truth I had never expected the biography of Stephen Crane to appear in my lifetime. My immense pleasure was affected by the devastating touch of time which like a muddy flood covers under a mass of daily trivialities things of value: moments of affectionate communion with kindred spirits, words spoken with the careless freedom of perfect confidence, the deepest emotions of joy and sorrow—together with such things of merely historical importance as the recollection of dates, for instance. After hearing from Mr. Beer of his difficulties in fixing certain dates in the history of Stephen Crane's life, I discovered that I was unable to remember with any kind of precision the initial date of our friendship. Indeed, life is but a dream—especially for those of us who have never kept a diary or possessed a notebook in our lives.

In this extremity I had recourse to another friend of Stephen Crane, who had appreciated him intuitively almost as soon as I did myself and who is a woman of excellent memory. My wife's recollection is that Crane and I met in London in October, 1897, and that he came to see us for the first time in our Essex home in the following November.

I have mentioned in a short paper written two years ago that it was Mr. S. S. Pawling, partner in the publishing firm of Mr. Heinemann, who brought us together. It was done at Stephen Crane's own desire.

I was told by Mr. Pawling that when asked whom he wanted to meet Crane mentioned two names, of which one was of a notable journalist (who had written some novels) whom he knew in America, I believe, and the other was mine. At that time the only facts we knew about each other were that we both had the same publisher in England. The only other fact I knew about Stephen Crane was that he was quite a young man. I had, of course, read his "Red Badge of Courage," of which people were writing and talking at that time. I certainly did not know that he had the slightest notion of my existence, or that he had seen a single line (there were not many of them then) of my writing. I can safely say that I earned this precious friendship by something like ten months of strenuous work with my pen. It took me just that time to write "The Nigger of the *Narcissus*," working at what I always considered a very high pressure. It was on the ground of the authorship of that book that Crane wanted to meet me. Nothing could have been more flattering than to discover that the author of "The Red Badge of Courage" appreciated my effort to present a group of men held together by a common loyalty and a common perplexity in a struggle not with human enemies, but with the hostile conditions testing their faithfulness to the conditions of their own calling.

Apart from the imaginative analysis of his own temperament tried by the emotions of a battlefield,

Stephen Crane dealt in his book with the psychology of the mass—the army; while I—in mine—had been dealing with the same subject on a much smaller scale and in more specialized conditions—the crew of a merchant ship, brought to the test of what I may venture to call the moral problem of conduct. This may be thought a very remote connection between these two works and the idea may seem too far-fetched to be mentioned here; but that was my undoubted feeling at the time. It is a fact that I considered Crane, by virtue of his creative experience with "The Red Badge of Courage," as eminently fit to pronounce a judgment on my first consciously planned attempt to render the truth of a phase of life in the terms of my own temperament with all the sincerity of which I was capable.

I had, of course, my own opinion as to what I had done; but I doubted whether anything of my ambitiously comprehensive aim would be understood. I was wrong there; but my doubt was excusable, since I myself would have been hard put to it if requested to give my complex intentions the form of a concise and definite statement. In that period of misgivings which so often follows an accomplished task I would often ask myself, who in the world could be interested in such a thing? It was after reading "The Red Badge," which came into my hands directly after its publication in England, that I said to myself: "Here's a man who may understand—if he ever sees the book; though of course that would not mean that he would like it." I do not mean to say that I looked towards the author of "The Red Badge" as the only man in the world. It would have been stupid and ungrateful. I had the moral support of one or two intimate friends and the solid fact of Mr. W. E. Henley's acceptance of my tale for serial publication in the *New Review* to give me confidence, while I awaited the larger verdict.

It seems to me that in trying to recall my memories of Stephen Crane I have been talking so far only about myself; but that is unavoidable, since this Introduction, which I am privileged to write, can only trace what is left on earth of our personal intercourse, which was even more short and fleeting than it may appear from the record of dates. October, 1897—May, 1900. And out of that beggarly tale of months must be deducted the time of his absence from England during the Spanish-American War, and of his visit to the United States shortly before the beginning of his last illness. Even when he was in England our intercourse was not so close and frequent as the warmth of our friendship would have wished it to be. We both lived in the country and, though not very far from each other, in different counties. I had my work to do, always in conditions which made it a matter of urgency. He had his own tasks and his own visions to attend to. I do not think that he had more friendships to claim him than I, but he certainly had more acquaintances and more calls on his time.

This was only natural. It must be remembered that as an author he was my senior, as I used to remind him now and then with affected humility which always provoked his smiles. He had a quiet smile that charmed and frightened one. It made you pause by something revelatory it cast over his whole physiognomy, not like a ray but like a shadow. I often asked myself what it could be, that quality that checked one's care-free mood, and now I think I have had my answer. It was the smile of a man who knows that his time will not be long on this earth.

I would not for a moment wish to convey the impression of melancholy in connection with my memories of Stephen Crane. I saw his smile first over the tablecloth in a restaurant. We shook hands with intense gravity and a direct stare at each other, after the manner of two children told to make friends. It was under the encouraging gaze of Sydney Pawling, who, a much bigger man than either of us and possessed of a deep voice, looked like a grown-up person entertaining two strange small boys—protecting and slightly anxious as to the experiment. He knew very little of either of us. I was a new author and Crane was a new arrival. It was the meeting of "The Red Badge" and "The Nigger" in the presence of their publisher; but as far as our personalities went we were three strangers breaking bread together for the first time. Yet it was as pleasantly easy a meal as any I can remember. Crane talked in his characteristic deliberate manner about Greece at war. I had already sensed the man's intense earnestness underlying his quiet surface. Every time he raised his eyes, that secret quality (for his voice was careless) of his soul was betrayed in a clear flash. Most of the true Stephen Crane was in his eyes, most of his strength at any rate, though it was apparent also in his other features, as, for instance, in the structure of his forehead, the deep solid arches under the fair eyebrows.

Some people saw traces of weakness in the lower part of his face. What I could see there was a hint of the delicacy of sentiment, of the inborn fineness of nature which this man, whose life had been anything but a stroll through a rose-garden, had managed to preserve like a sacred heritage. I say heritage, not acquisition, for it was not and could not have been acquired. One could depend on it on all occasions; whereas the cultivated kind is apt to show ugly gaps under very slight

provocation. The coarseness of the professedly delicate must be very amusing to the misanthrope. But
Crane was no enemy of his kind. That sort of thing
did not amuse him. As to his own temper, it was proof
against anger and scorn, as I can testify, having seen
him both angry and scornful, always quietly, on
fitting occasions. Contempt and indignation never
broke the surface of his moderation, simply because
he had no surface. He was all through of the same
material, incapable of affectation of any kind, of any
pitiful failure of generosity for the sake of personal
advantage, or even from sheer exasperation which must
find its relief.

Many people imagined him a fiery individuality.
Certainly he was not cold-blooded. But his was an
equable glow, morally and temperamentally. I would
have said the same of his creative power (I have seen
him sit down before a blank sheet of paper, dip his pen,
write the first line at once and go on without haste and
without pause for a couple of hours), had he not con-
fided to me that his mentality did flag at times. I do
not think it was anything more than every writer is
familiar with at times. Another man would have
talked of his "failing inspiration." It is very characteristic of Crane that I have never heard him use that
word when talking about his work.

His phraseology was generally of a very modest cast.
That unique and exquisite faculty, which Edward
Garnett, another of his friends, found in his writing—
"of disclosing an individual scene by an odd simile"—
was not apparent in his conversation. It was interesting, of course, but its charm consisted mainly in the
freshness of his impressions, set off by an acute simplicity of view and expressed with an amusing de-
liberation. Superabundance of words was not his

failing when communing with those he liked and felt he could trust. With the other kind of "friends" he followed the method of a sort of suspended silence. On a certain occasion (it was at Brede Place), after two amazingly conceited idiots had gone away, I said to him, "Stevie, you brood like a distant thundercloud." He had retired early to the other end of the room, and from there had sent out, now and then, a few words, more like the heavy drops of rain that precede the storm than growls of thunder. Poor Crane, if he could look black enough at times, never thundered; though I have no doubt he could have been dangerous if he had liked. There always seemed to be something (not timidity) which restrained him, not from within but, I could not help fancying, from outside, with an effect as of a whispered *memento mori* in the ear of a reveller not lost to the sense of grace.

That of course was a later impression. It must be stated clearly that I know very little of Stephen Crane's life. We did not feel the need to tell each other formally the story of our lives. That did not prevent us from being very intimate and also very open with each other from the first. Our affection would have been "everlasting," as he himself qualified it, had not the jealous death intervened with her cruel capriciousness by striking down the younger man. Our intimacy was really too close to admit of indiscretions; not that he did not speak amusingly of his experiences and of his hardships, and warmly of the men that helped him in his early days, like Mr. Hamlin Garland for instance, or men kindly encouraging to him, like Mr. Howells. Many other names he used to utter lovingly have been forgotten by me after so many years.

It is a fact that I heard more of his adventures than of his trials, privations, and difficulties. I know he had many. He was the least recriminatory of men (though one of the most sensitive, I should say), but, in any case, nothing I could have learned would have shaken the independent judgment I had formed for myself of his trustworthiness as a man and a friend. Though the word is discredited now and may sound pretentious, I will say that there was in Crane a strain of chivalry which made him safe to trust with one's life. To be recognizably a man of honour carries no immunity against human weaknesses, but comports more rigid limitations in personal relations than the status of an "honourable man," however recognizable that too may be. Some men are "honourable" by courtesy, others by the office they hold, or simply by belonging to some popular assembly, the election to which is not generally secured by a dignified accuracy of statement and a scrupulous regard for the feelings of others. Many remain honourable (because of their great circumspection in the conduct of their affairs) without holding within themselves any of these restraints which are inherent in the character of a man of honour, however weak or luckless he may be.

I do not know everything about the strength of Crane's circumspection, but I am not afraid of what the biography which follows may disclose to us; though I am convinced that it will be free from hypocritical reservations. I think I have understood Stephen Crane, and from my too short acquaintance with his biographer I am confident he will receive the most humane and sympathetic treatment. What I discovered very early in our acquaintance was that Crane had not the face of a lucky man. That certitude came to me at our first meeting while I sat opposite him listening to his simple tales of Greece, while S. S. Pawling presided at the initiatory feast—friendly and debonair, looking solidly anchored in the stream of life, and very reassuring, like a big, prosperous ship to the sides of which we two in our tossing little barks could hook on for safety. He was interested in the tales too; and the best proof of it is that when he looked at his watch and jumped up, saying, "I must leave you two now," it was very near four o'clock. Nearly a whole afternoon wasted, for an English business man.

No such consideration of waste or duty agitated Crane and myself. The sympathy that, even in regard of the very few years allotted to our friendship, may be said to have sprung up instantaneously between us, was the most undemonstrative case of that sort in the last century. We not only did not tell each other of it (which would have been missish), but even without entering formally into a previous agreement to remain together, we went out and began to walk side by side in the manner of two tramps without home, occupation, or care for the next night's shelter. We certainly paid no heed to direction. The first thing I noticed were the Green Park railings, when to my remark that he had seen no war before he went to Greece, Crane made answer: "No. But 'The Red Badge' is all right." I assured him that I never had doubted it; and, since the title of the work had been pronounced for the first time, feeling I must do something to show I had read it, I said shyly: "I like your General." He knew at once what I was alluding to, but said not a word. Nothing could have been more tramp-like than our silent pacing, elbow to elbow, till, after we had left Hyde Park Corner behind us, Crane uttered with his quiet earnestness the words: "I like your young man— I can just see him." Nothing could have been more characteristic of the depth of our three-hour-old intimacy than that each of us should have selected for praise the merest by-the-way vignette of a minor character.

This was positively the only allusion we made that afternoon to our immortal works. Indeed we talked very little of them at any time, and then always selecting some minor point for particular mention; which, after all, is not a bad way of showing an affectionate appreciation of a piece of work done by a friend. A stranger would have expected more, but, in a manner of speaking, Crane and I had never been strangers. We took each other's work for granted from the very first, I mean from the moment we had exchanged those laudatory remarks alongside the Green Park railings. Henceforth mutual recognition kept to that standard. It consisted often of an approving grunt, sometimes of the mention of some picked-out paragraph, or of a line or only of a few words that had caught our fancy and would, for a time, be applied more or less aptly to the turns of our careless, or even serious, talks.

Thus, for instance, there was a time when I persecuted poor Crane with the words "barbarously abrupt." They occur in that marvellous story, "The Open Boat", and are applied by him to the waves of the sea (as seen by men tossing in a small dinghy) with an inspired audacity of epithet which was one of Crane's gifts that gave me most delight. How amazingly apt these words are where they stand, anybody can see by looking at that story, which is altogether a big thing, and has remained an object of my confirmed admiration. I was always telling Crane that this or that was "barbarously abrupt," or begging him not to be so "barbarously abrupt" himself, with a keen enjoyment of the incongruity; for no human being could be less abrupt than Crane. As to his humanity (in contradistinction to barbarity), it was a shining thing without a flaw. It is possible that he may have grown at length weary of my little joke, but he invariably received it with a smile, thus proving his consistent humanity towards his kind. But, after all, he too liked that story of his, of four men in a very small boat, which by the deep and simple humanity of presentation seems somehow to illustrate the essentials of life itself, like a symbolic tale. It opens with a phrase that anybody could have uttered, but which, in relation to what is to follow, acquires the poignancy of a meaning almost universal. Once, much later in our acquaintance, I made use of it to him. He came on a flying visit to Pent Farm where we were living then. I noticed that he looked harassed. I, too, was feeling for the moment as if things were getting too much for me. He lay on the couch and I sat on a chair opposite. After a longish silence, in which we both could have felt how uncertain was the issue of life envisaged as a deadly adventure in which we were both engaged like two men trying to keep afloat in a small boat, I said suddenly across the width of the mantelpiece:

"None of them knew the colour of the sky."

He raised himself sharply. The words had struck him as familiar, though I believe he failed to place them at first. "Don't you know that quotation?" I asked. (These words form the opening sentence of his tale.) The startled expression passed off his face. "Oh, yes," he said quietly, and lay down again. Truth to say, it was a time when neither he nor I had the leisure to look up idly at the sky. The waves just then were too "barbarously abrupt."

I do not mean to say that it was always so. Now and then we were permitted to snatch a glance at the colour of the sky. But it is a fact that in the history of our essentially undemonstrative friendship (which is nearly as difficult to recapture as a dream) that first long afternoon is the most care-free instant, and the only one that had a character of enchantment about it. It was spread out over a large portion of central London. After the Green Park the next thing I remember are the Kensington Gardens, where under the lofty and historical trees I was vouchsafed a glimpse of the low mesquite bush overspreading the plum-coloured infinities of the great Texas plains. Then after a long tramp amongst an orderly multitude of grimy brick houses—from which the only things I carried off were the impressions of the coloured rocks of Mexico (or was it Arizona?), and my first knowledge of a locality called the Painted Desert—there came suddenly Oxford Street. I don't know whether the inhabitants of London were keeping indoors or had gone into the country that afternoon, but I don't remember seeing any people in the streets except for a figure, now and then, unreal, flitting by, obviously negligible. The wheeled traffic, too, was stopped; yet, it seems, not entirely, because I remember Crane seizing my arm and jerking me back on the pavement with the calm remark: "You will get run over." I love to think that the dear fellow had saved my life and that it seemed to amuse him. As to London's enormous volume of business, all I know is that one A. B. C. shop had remained open. We went through the depressing ceremony of having tea there; but our interest in each other mitigated its inherent horrors and gave me a good idea of Crane's stoicism. At least I suppose we had tea, otherwise they would not have let us sit there so long. To be left alone was all we wanted. Neither of us had then a club to entertain the other in. It will give a good notion of our indomitable optimism (on that afternoon) when I say that it was there, in those dismal surroundings, we reached the conclusion that though the world had grown old and weary, yet the scheme of creation remained as obscure as ever, and (from our own particular point of view) there was still much that was interesting to expect from gods and men.

As if intoxicated by this draught of hope we rolled out of that A. B. C. shop, but I kept my head sufficiently to guess what was coming and to send a warning telegram to my wife in our Essex home. Crane then was, I believe, staying temporarily in London. But he seemed to have no care in the world; and so we resumed our tramping—east and north and south again, steering through uncharted mazes the streets, forgetting to think of dinner but taking a rest here and there, till we found ourselves, standing in the middle of Piccadilly Circus, blinking at the lights like two authentic nightbirds. By that time we had been (in Tottenham Court Road) joined by Balzac. How he came in I have no idea. Crane was not given to literary curiosities of that kind. Somebody he knew, or something he had read, must have attracted lately his attention to Balzac. And now suddenly at ten o'clock in the evening he demanded insistently to be told in particular detail all about the "Comédie Humaine," its contents, its scope, its plan, and its general significance, together with a critical description of Balzac's style. I told him hastily that it was just black on white; and for the rest, I said, he would have to wait till we got across to Monico's and had eaten some supper. I hoped he would forget Balzac and his "Comédie." But not a bit of it; and I had no option but to hold forth over the remnants of a meal, in the rush of hundreds of waiters and the clatter of tons of crockery, caring not what I said (for what could Stephen want with Balzac?), in the comfortable

assurance that the Monstrous Shade, even if led by
some strange caprice to haunt the long room of Monico's,
did not know enough English to understand a single
word I said. I wonder what Crane made of it all. He
did not look bored, and it was eleven o'clock before we
parted at the foot of that monumentally heavy abode
of frivolity, the Pavilion, with just a hand-shake and a
good-night—no more—without making any arrangements for meeting again, as though we had lived in the
same town from childhood and were sure to run across
each other next day.

It struck me directly I left him that we had not even
exchanged addresses; but I was not uneasy. Sure
enough, before the month was out there arrived a post
card (from Ravensbrook) asking whether he might
come to see us. He came, was received as an old friend,
and before the end of the day conquered my wife's
sympathy, as undemonstrative and sincere as his own
quiet friendliness. The friendship that sprang up between them was confirmed by the interest Crane displayed in our first child, a boy who came on the scene
not quite two months afterwards. How strong was that
interest on the part of Stephen Crane and his wife in the
boy is evidenced by the fact that at the age of six weeks
he was invited to come for a long visit to Ravensbrook.
He was in fact impatiently expected there. He arrived
in state, bringing with him not only his parents but also
a young aunt, and was welcomed like a prince. This
visit, during which I suffered from a sense of temporary
extinction, is commemorated by a group photograph
taken by an artist summoned with his engine (regardless
of expense) to Ravensbrook. Though the likenesses
are not bad, it is a very awful thing. Nobody looks
like him or herself in it. The best yet are the Crane
dogs, a very important part of the establishment and

quite conscious of it, belonging apparently to some order of outlandish poodles, amazingly sedate, and yet the most restless animals I have ever met. They pervaded, populated, and filled the whole house. Whichever way one looked at any time, down the passage, up the stairs, into the drawing room, there was always a dog in sight. Had I been asked on the first day how many there were, I would have guessed about thirty. As a matter of fact there were only three, but I think they never sat down, except in Crane's study, where they had their *entrée* at all hours.

A scratching would be heard at the door, Crane would drop his pen with alacrity to throw it open—and the dogs would enter sedately in single file, taking a lot of time about it, too. Then the room would resound for a while with grunts, sniffs, yawns, heavy flops, followed by as much perhaps as three whole minutes of silence. Then the dogs would get up, one after another, never all together, and direct their footsteps to the door in an impressive and ominous manner. The first arrival waited considerately for the others before trying to attract attention by means of scratching on the bottom panel. Then, never before, Crane would raise his head, go meekly to the door—and the procession would file out at the slowest possible pace. The recurrent sedateness of the proceedings, the utter unconsciousness of the dogs, dear Stephen's absurd gravity while playing his part in those ceremonies, without ever a muscle of his face moving, were irresistibly, exasperatingly funny. I tried to preserve my gravity (or at least to keep calm), with fair success. Only one afternoon on the fifth or sixth repetition I could not help bursting into a loud interminable laugh, and then the dear fellow asked me in all innocence what was the matter. I managed to conceal my nervous irritation from him, and he never learned the secret of that laugh in which there was a beginning of hysteria.

If the definition that man is a laughing animal be true, then Crane was neither one nor the other; indeed he was but a hurried visitor on this earth on which he had so little reason to be joyous. I might say that I never heard him laugh, except in connection with the baby. He loved children; but his friendship with our child was of the kind that put our mutual sentiment, by comparison, somewhere within the arctic region. The two could not be compared; at least I have never detected Crane stretched full length and sustained on his elbows on a grass plot, in order to gaze at me; on the other hand, this was his usual attitude of communion with the small child—with him who was called *the Boy* and whose destiny it was to see more war before he came of age than the author of "The Red Badge" had time to see in all the allotted days of his life. In the gravity of its disposition the baby came quite up to Crane; yet those two would sometimes find something to laugh at in each other. Then there would be silence, and glancing out of the low window of my room I would see them, very still, staring at each other with a solemn understanding that needed no words, or perhaps was beyond words altogether. I could not object on any ground to their profound intimacy, but I do not see why Crane should have developed such an unreasonable suspicion as to my paternal efficiency. He seemed to be everlastingly taking the boy's part. I could not see that the baby was being oppressed, hectored over, or in any way deprived of its rights, or ever wounded in its feelings by me; but Crane seemed always to nurse some vague unexpressed grievance as to my conduct. I was inconsiderate. For instance—why could I not get a dog for the boy? One day he made quite a scene about it. He seemed to imply I should drop everything and go look for a dog. I sat under the storm and said nothing. At last he cried, "Hang it all, a boy ought to have a dog." It was an appeal to first principles, but for an answer I pointed at the window and said: "Behold the boy." . . . He was sitting on a rug spread on the grass, with his little red stocking-cap very much over one eye (a fact of which he seemed unaware), and propped round with many pillows on account of his propensity to roll over on his side helplessly. My answer was irresistible. This is one of the few occasions on which I heard Stephen Crane laugh outright. He dropped his preaching on the dog theme and went out to the boy while I went on with my work. But he was strangely incorrigible. When he came back after an hour or so, his first words were, "Joseph, I will teach your boy to ride." I closed with the offer at once—but it was not to be. He was not given the time.

The happiest mental picture my wife and I preserve of Crane is on the occasion of our first visit to Brede Place when he rode to meet us at the Park gate. He looked at his best on horseback. On that day he must have been feeling well. As usual, he was happy in the saddle. As he went on trotting by the side of the open trap I said to him: "If you give the boy your seat I will be perfectly satisfied." I knew this would please him; and indeed his face remained wreathed in smiles all the way to the front door. He looked about him at that bit of the world, down the green slopes and up the brown fields, with an appreciative serenity and the confident bearing of a man who is feeling very sure of the present and of the future. All because he was looking at life from the saddle, with a good morning's work behind him. Nothing more is needed to give a man a blessed moment of illusion. The more I think of that morning, the more I believe it was just that; that it had really been given me to see Crane perfectly happy for a couple of hours; and that it was under this spell that directly we arrived he led me impatiently to the room in which he worked when at Brede. After we got there he said to me, "Joseph, I will give you something." I had no idea what it would be, till I saw him sit down to write an inscription in a very slim volume. He presented it to me with averted head. It was "The Black Riders." He had never spoken to me of his verse before. It was while holding the book in my hand that I learned that they were written years before in America. I expressed my appreciation of them that afternoon in the usual half-a-dozen, or dozen, words which we allowed ourselves when completely pleased with each other's work. When the pleasure was not so complete the words would be many. And that was a great waste of breath and time. I must confess that we were no critics, I mean temperamentally. Crane was even less of a critic than myself. Criticism is very much a matter of a vocabulary, very consciously used; with us it was the intonation that mattered. The tone of a grunt could convey an infinity of meaning between us.

The articulate literary conscience at our elbow was Edward Garnett. He, of course, was worth listening to. His analytical appreciation (or appreciative analysis) of Crane's art, in the London *Academy* of 17th December, 1898,[1] goes to the root of the matter with Edward's almost uncanny insight, and a well-balanced sympathy with the blind, pathetic striving of the artist towards a complete realization of his individual gift. How highly Edward Garnett rated Crane's gift is recorded in the conclusions of that admirable and,

---

[1] Extended and republished in the volume "Friday Nights."

within the limits of its space, masterly article of some
two columns, where at the end are set down such
affirmative phrases as: "The chief impressionist of the
age." . . . "Mr. Crane's talent is unique" . . .
and where he hails him as "the creator of fresh rhythms
and phrases," while the very last words state confidently
that: "Undoubtedly, of the young school it is Mr. Crane
who is the genius—the others have their talents."

My part here being not that of critic but of private
friend, all I will say is that I agreed warmly at the
time with that article, which from the quoted phrases
might be supposed a merely enthusiastic pronounce-
ment, but on reading will be found to be based on that
calm sagacity which Edward Garnett, for all his fiery
zeal in the cause of letters, could always summon for the
judgment of matters emotional—as all response to the
various forms of art must be in the main. I had
occasion to re-read it last year in its expanded form in a
collection of literary essays of great, now almost historical, interest in the record of American and English
imaginative literature. I found there a passage or two,
not bearing precisely on Crane's work but giving a view
of his temperament, on which of course his art was
based; and of the conditions, moral and material, under
which he had to put forth his creative faculties and his
power of steady composition. Of those matters, as a
man who had the opportunity to look at Crane's life
in England, I wish to offer a few remarks before closing
my contribution to the memory of my friend.

I do not know that he was ever dunned for money
and had to work under a threat of legal proceedings.
I don't think he was ever dunned in the sense in which
such a phrase is used about a spendthrift unscrupulous
in incurring debts. No doubt he was sometimes pressed

for money. He lived by his pen, and the prices he obtained were not great. Personally he was not extravagant; and I will not quarrel with him for not choosing to live in a garret. The tenancy of Brede Place was held by him at a nominal rent. That glorious old place was not restored then, and the greatest part of it was uninhabitable. The Cranes had furnished in a modest way six or seven of the least dilapidated rooms, which even then looked bare and half empty. Certainly there was a horse, and at one time even two, but that luxury was not so very expensive at that time. One man looked after them. Riding was the only exercise open to Crane; and if he did work so hard, surely he was entitled to some relaxation, if only for the preservation of his unique talent.

His greatest extravagance was hospitality, of which I, too, had my share; often in the company, I am sorry to say, of men who after sitting at his board chose to speak of him and of his wife slightingly. Having some rudimentary sense of decency, their behaviour while actually under the Cranes' roof often produced on me a disagreeable impression. Once I ventured to say to him, "You are too good-natured, Stephen." He gave me one of his quiet smiles, that seemed to hint so poignantly at the vanity of all things, and after a period of silence remarked: "I am glad those Indians are gone." He was surrounded by men who, secretly envious, hostile to the real quality of his genius (and a little afraid of it), were also in antagonism with the essential fineness of his nature. But enough of them. *Pulvis et umbra sunt.* I mean even those that may be alive yet. They were ever hardly anything else; one would have forgotten them if it were not for the legend (if one may dignify perfidious and contemptible gossip by that name) they created in order to satisfy that same obscure instinct of base humanity, which in the past would often bring against any exceptional man the charge of consorting with the devil. It was just as vague, just as senseless, and in its implications just as lying as the mediæval kind. I have heard one of these "friends" hint before several other Philistines that Crane could not write his tales without getting drunk!

Putting aside the gross palpable stupidity of such a statement—which the creature gave out as an instance of the artistic temperament—I am in a position to disclose what may have been the foundation of this piece of gossip. I have seen repeatedly Crane at work. A small jug of still smaller ale would be brought into the study at about ten o'clock; Crane would pour out some of it into a glass and settle himself at the long table at which he used to write in Brede Place. I would take a book and settle myself at the other end of the same table, with my back to him; and for two hours or so not a sound would be heard in that room. At the end of that time Crane would say suddenly: "I won't do any more now, Joseph." He would have covered three of his large sheets with his regular, legible, perfectly controlled handwriting, with no more than a half-a-dozen erasures—mostly single words—in the whole lot. It seemed to me always a perfect miracle in the way of mastery over material and expression. Most of the ale would be still in the glass, and how flat by that time I don't like to think! The most amusing part was to see Crane, as if moved by some obscure sense of duty, drain the last drop of that untempting remnant before we left the room to stroll to and fro in front of the house while waiting for lunch. Such is the origin of some of these gleeful whispers making up the Crane legend of "unrestrained temperament." I have known various sorts of temperaments—some perfidious and some lying—

but "unrestrained temperament" is mere parrot talk. It has no meaning. But it was suggestive. It was founded on Crane's visits to town, during which I more than once met him there. We used to spend afternoons and evenings together, and I did not see any of his supposed revels in progress; nor yet have I ever detected any after effects of them on any occasion. Neither have I ever seen anybody who would own to having been a partner in those excesses—if only to the extent of standing by charitably—which would have been a noble part to play. I daresay all those "excesses" amounted to very little more than the one in which he asked me to join him in the following letter. It is the only note I have kept from the very few which we exchanged. The reader will see why it is one of my most carefully preserved possessions.

RAVENSBROOK, OXTED,
March 17 (1899).

MY DEAR CONRAD:

I am enclosing you a bit of MS. under the supposition that you might like to keep it in remembrance of my warm and endless friendship for you. I am still hoping that you will consent to Stokes' invitation to come to the Savage on Saturday night. Cannot you endure it? Give my affectionate remembrances to Mrs. Conrad and my love to the boy.

Yours always,
STEPHEN CRANE.

P. S. You must accept says Cora—and I—our invitation to come home with me on Sat. night.

I joined him. We had a very amusing time with the Savages. Afterwards Crane refused to go home till the last train. Evidence of what somebody has called his "unrestrained temperament," no doubt. So we went and sat at Gatti's, I believe—unless it was in a Bodega which existed then in that neighbourhood—and talked. I have a vivid memory of this awful debauch because it was on that evening that Crane told me of a subject for a story—a very exceptional thing for him to do. He called it "The Predecessor." I could not recall now by what capricious turns and odd associations of thought he reached the enthusiastic conclusion that it would make a good play, and that we must do it together. He wanted me to share in a certain success—"a dead sure thing," he said. His was an unrestrainedly generous temperament. But let that pass. I must have been specially predisposed, because I caught the infection at once. There and then we began to build up the masterpiece, interrupting each other eagerly, for, I don't know how it was, the air around us had suddenly grown thick with felicitous suggestions. We carried on this collaboration as far as the railway time-table would let us, and then made a break for the last train. Afterwards we did talk of our collaboration now and then, but no attempt at it was ever made. Crane had other stories to write; I was immersed deeply in "Lord Jim," of which I had to keep up the instalments in *Blackwood's;* difficulties in presenting the subject on the stage rose one after another before our experience. The general subject consisted in a man personating his "predecessor" (who had died) in the hope of winning a girl's heart. The scenes were to include a ranch at the foot of the Rocky Mountains, I remember, and the action, I fear, would have been frankly melodramatic. Crane insisted that one of the situations should present the man and the girl on a boundless plain standing by their dead ponies after a furious ride (a truly Crane touch). I made some objections. A boundless plain in the light of a sunset could be got into a back-cloth, I admitted; but I doubted whether we could induce the management of any London theatre to deposit two stuffed horses on its stage.

Recalling now those earnestly fantastic discussions, it occurs to me that Crane and I must have been unconsciously penetrated by a prophetic sense of the technique and of the very spirit of film-plays, of which even the name was unknown then to the world. But if gifted with prophetic sense, we must have been strangely ignorant of ourselves, since it must be obvious to any one who has read a page of our writings that a collaboration between us two could never have come to anything in the end—could never even have been begun. The project was merely the expression of our affection for each other. We were fascinated for a moment by the will-of-the-wisp of close artistic communion. It would in no case have led us into a bog. I flatter myself we both had too much regard for each other's gifts not to be clear-eyed about them. We would not have followed the lure very far. At the same time it cannot be denied that there were profound, if not extensive, similitudes in our temperaments which could create for a moment that fascinating illusion. It is not to be regretted, for it had, at any rate, given us some of the most light-hearted moments in the clear but sober atmosphere of our intimacy. From the force of circumstances there could not be much sunshine in it. "None of them saw the colour of the sky!" And alas, it stood already written that it was the younger man who would fail to make a landing through the surf. So I am glad to have that episode to remember, a brotherly serio-comic interlude, played under the shadow of coming events. But I would not have alluded to it at all if it had not come out in the course of my most interesting talk with the author of this biography, that Crane had thought it worth while to mention it in his correspondence, whether seriously or humorously, I know not. So here it is without the charm which it had for me, but which cannot be reproduced in the mere relation of its outward characteristics: a clear gleam on us two, succeeded by the Spanish-American War into which Crane disappeared like a wilful man walking away into the depths of an ominous twilight.

The cloudy afternoon when we two went rushing all over London together was for him the beginning of the end. The problem was to find £60 that day, before the sun set, before dinner, before the "six-forty" train to Oxted, at once, that instant—lest peace should be declared and the opportunity of seeing a war be missed. I had not £60 to lend him. Sixty shillings was nearer my mark. We tried various offices but had no luck, or rather we had the usual luck of money-hunting enterprises. The man was either gone out to see about a dog, or would take no interest in the Spanish-American War. In one place the man wanted to know what was the hurry? He would have liked to have forty-eight hours to think the matter over. As we came downstairs, Crane's white-faced excitement frightened me. Finally it occurred to me to take him to Messrs. William Blackwood & Sons' London office. There he was received in a most friendly way. Presently I escorted him to Charing Cross, where he took the train for home with the assurance that he would have the means to start "for the war" next day. That is the reason I cannot to this day read his tale, "The Price of the Harness", without a pang. It has done nothing more deadly than pay his debt to Messrs. Blackwood;

yet now and then I feel as though that afternoon I had led him by the hand to his doom. But, indeed, I was only the blind agent of the fate that had him in her grip! Nothing could have held him back. He was ready to swim the ocean.

Thirteen years afterwards I made use, half consciously, of the shadow of the primary idea of "The Predecessor" in one of my short tales which were serialized in the *Metropolitan Magazine*. But in that tale the dead man in the background is not a Predecessor but merely an assistant on a lonely plantation; and instead of the ranch, the mountains, and the plains, there is a cloud-capped island, a bird-haunted reef, and the sea. All this the mere distorted shadow of what we two used to talk about in a fantastic mood; but now and then, as I wrote, I had the feeling that he had the right to come and look over my shoulder. But he never came. I received no suggestions from him, subtly conveyed without words. There will never be any collaboration for us now. But I wonder, were he alive, whether he would be pleased with the tale. I don't know. Perhaps not. Or, perhaps, after picking up the volume with that detached air I remember so well and turning over page after page in silence, he would suddenly read aloud a line or two and then, looking straight into my eyes as was his wont on such occasions, say with all the intense earnestness of affection that was in him: "I—like—that, Joseph."

HIS WAR BOOK

A Preface to Stephen Crane's "The Red Badge of Courage"

ONE of the most enduring memories of my literary life is the sensation produced by the appearance in 1895 of Crane's "Red Badge of Courage" in a small volume belonging to Mr. Heinemann's Pioneer Series of Modern Fiction—very modern fiction of that time, and upon the whole not devoid of merit. I have an idea the series was meant to give us shocks, and as far as my recollection goes there were, to use a term made familiar to all by another war, no "duds" in that small and lively bombardment. But Crane's work detonated on the mild din of that attack on our literary sensibilities with the impact and force of a twelve-inch shell charged with a very high explosive. Unexpected it fell amongst us; and its fall was followed by a great outcry.

Not of consternation, however. The energy of that projectile hurt nothing and no one (such was its good fortune), and delighted a good many. It delighted soldiers, men of letters, men in the street; it was welcomed by all lovers of personal expression as a genuine revelation, satisfying the curiosity of a world in which war and love have been subjects of song and story ever since the beginning of articulate speech.

Here we had an artist, a man not of experience but a man inspired, a seer with a gift for rendering the significant on the surface of things and with an incomparable insight into primitive emotions, who, in order to give

119

us the image of war, had looked profoundly into his own breast. We welcomed him. As if the whole vocabulary of praise had been blown up sky-high by this missile from across the Atlantic, a rain of words descended on our heads, words well or ill chosen, chunks of pedantic praise and warm appreciation, clever words, and words of real understanding, platitudes, and felicities of criticism, but all as sincere in their response as the striking piece of work which set so many critical pens scurrying over the paper.

One of the most interesting, if not the most valuable, of printed criticisms was perhaps that of Mr. George Wyndham, soldier, man of the world, and in a sense a man of letters. He went into the whole question of war literature, at any rate during the nineteenth century, evoking comparisons with the *Mémoires* of General Marbot and the famous *Diary of a Cavalry Officer* as records of a personal experience. He rendered justice to the interest of what soldiers themselves could tell us, but confessed that to gratify the curiosity of the potential combatant who lurks in most men as to the picturesque aspects and emotional reactions of a battle we must go to the artist with his Heaven-given faculty of words at the service of his divination as to what the truth of things is and must be. He comes to the conclusion that:

"Mr. Crane has contrived a masterpiece."

"Contrived"—that word of disparaging sound is the last word I would have used in connection with any piece of work by Stephen Crane, who in his art (as indeed in his private life) was the least "contriving" of men. But as to "masterpiece," there is no doubt that "The Red Badge of Courage" is that, if only because of the marvellous accord of the vivid impressionistic description of action on that woodland battlefield, and the imaged style of the analysis of the emotions in the inward moral struggle going on in the breast of one individual—the Young Soldier of the book, the protagonist of the monodrama presented to us in an effortless succession of graphic and coloured phrases.

Stephen Crane places his Young Soldier in an untried regiment. And this is well contrived—if any contrivance there be in a spontaneous piece of work which seems to spurt and flow like a tapped stream from the depths of the writer's being. In order that the revelation should be complete, the Young Soldier has to be deprived of the moral support which he would have found in a tried body of men matured in achievement to the consciousness of its worth. His regiment had been tried by nothing but days of waiting for the order to move; so many days that it and the Youth within it have come to think of themselves as merely "a part of a vast blue demonstration." The army had been lying camped near a river, idle and fretting, till the moment when Stephen Crane lays hold of it at dawn with masterly simplicity: "The cold passed reluctantly from the earth. . . ." These are the first words of the war book which was to give him his crumb of fame.

The whole of that opening paragraph is wonderful in the homely dignity of the indicated lines of the landscape, and the shivering awakening of the army at the break of the day before the battle. In the next, with a most effective change to racy colloquialism of narrative, the action which motivates, sustains and feeds the inner drama forming the subject of the book, begins with the Tall Soldier going down to the river to wash his shirt. He returns waving his garment above his head. He had heard at fifth-hand from somebody that the army is going to move to-morrow. The only immediate effect of this piece of news is that a Negro teamster, who had

been dancing a jig on a wooden box in a ring of laughing
soldiers, finds himself suddenly deserted. He sits down
mournfully. For the rest, the Tall Soldier's excitement is met by blank disbelief, profane grumbling, an
invincible incredulity. But the regiment is somehow
sobered. One feels it, though no symptoms can be
noticed. It does not know what a battle is, neither does
the Young Soldier. He retires from the babbling throng
into what seems a rather comfortable dugout and lies
down with his hands over his eyes to think. Thus the
drama begins.

He perceives suddenly that he had looked upon wars
as historical phenomenons of the past. He had never
believed in war in his own country. It had been a sort
of play affair. He had been drilled, inspected, marched
for months, till he has despaired "of ever seeing a Greek-
like struggle. Such were no more. Men were better
or more timid. Secular and religious education had
effaced the throat-grappling instinct, or else firm finance
held in check the passions."

Very modern this touch. We can remember thoughts
like these round about the year 1914. That Young
Soldier is representative of mankind in more ways than
one, and first of all in his ignorance. His regiment had
listened to the tales of veterans, "tales of gray be-
whiskered hordes chewing tobacco with unspeakable
valour and sweeping along like the Huns." Still, he
cannot put his faith in veterans' tales. Recruits were
their prey. They talked of blood, fire, and sudden
death, but much of it might have been lies. They were
in no wise to be trusted. And the question arises
before him whether he will or will not "run from a
battle"? He does not know. He cannot know. A
little panic fear enters his mind. He jumps up and
asks himself aloud, "Good Lord, what's the matter

with me?" This is the first time his words are quoted, on this day before the battle. He dreads not danger, but fear itself. He stands before the unknown. He would like to prove to himself by some reasoning process that he will not "run from the battle." And in his unblooded regiment he can find no help. He is alone with the problem of courage.

In this he stands for the symbol of all untried men. Some critics have estimated him a morbid case. I cannot agree to that. The abnormal cases are of the extremes; of those who crumple up at the first sight of danger, and of those of whom their fellows say "He doesn't know what fear is." Neither will I forget the rare favourites of the gods whose fiery spirit is only soothed by the fury and clamour of a battle. Of such was General Picton of Peninsular fame. But the lot of the mass of mankind is to know fear, the decent fear of disgrace. Of such is the Young Soldier of "The Red Badge of Courage." He only seems exceptional because he has got inside of him Stephen Crane's imagination, and is presented to us with the insight and the power of expression of an artist whom a just and severe critic, on a review of all his work, has called the foremost impressionist of his time; as Sterne was the greatest impressionist, but in a different way, of his age.

This is a generalized, fundamental judgment. More superficially both Zola's "La Débâcle" and Tolstoi's "War and Peace" were mentioned by critics in connection with Crane's war book. But Zola's main concern was with the downfall of the imperial régime he fancied he was portraying; and in Tolstoi's book the subtle presentation of Rostov's squadron under fire for the first time is a mere episode lost in a mass of other matter, like a handful of pebbles in a heap of sand. I could not see the relevancy. Crane was concerned with elemental truth only; and in any case I think that as an artist he is non-comparable. He dealt with what is enduring, and was the most detached of men.

That is why his book is short. Not quite two hundred pages. Gems are small. This monodrama, which happy inspiration or unerring instinct has led him to put before us in narrative form, is contained between the opening words I have already quoted and a phrase on page 194 of the English edition, which runs: "He had been to touch the great death, and found that, after all, it was but the great death. He was a man."

On these words the action ends. We are only given one glimpse of the victorious army at dusk, under the falling rain, "a procession of weary soldiers became a bedraggled train, despondent and muttering, marching with churning effort in a trough of liquid brown mud under a low wretched sky . . .", while the last ray of the sun falls on the river through a break in the leaden clouds.

This war book, so virile and so full of gentle sympathy, in which not a single declamatory sentiment defaces the genuine verbal felicity, welding analysis and description in a continuous fascination of individual style, had been hailed by the critics as the herald of a brilliant career. Crane himself very seldom alluded to it, and always with a wistful smile. Perhaps he was conscious that, like the mortally wounded Tall Soldier of his book, who, snatching at the air, staggers out into a field to meet his appointed death on the first day of battle— while the terrified Youth and the kind Tattered Soldier stand by silent, watching with awe "these ceremonies at the place of meeting"—it was his fate, too, to fall early in the fray.

JOHN GALSWORTHY

When in the family's assembly at Timothy Forsyte's house there arose a discussion of Francie Forsyte's verses, Aunt Hester expressed her preference for the poetry of Shelley, Byron and Wordsworth, on the ground that, after reading the works of these poets, "one felt that one had read a book." And the reader of Mr. Galsworthy's latest volume of fiction, whether in accord or in difference with the author's view of his subject, would feel that he had read a book.

Beyond that impression one perceives how difficult it is to get critical hold of Mr. Galsworthy's work. He gives you no opening. Defending no obvious thesis, setting up no theory, offering no cheap panacea, appealing to no naked sentiment, the author of "The Man of Property" disdains also the effective device of attacking insidiously the actors of his own drama, or rather of his dramatic comedy. This is because he does not write for effect, though his writing will be found effective enough for all that. This book is of a disconcerting honesty, backed by a discouraging skill. There is not a single phrase in it written for the sake of its cleverness. Not one. Light of touch, though weighty in feeling, it gives the impression of verbal austerity, of a *willed* moderation of thought. The passages of high literary merit, so uniformly sustained as to escape the notice of the reader, expose the natural and logical development of the story with a purposeful progression which is primarily satisfying to the intelligence, and ends by stirring the emotions. In the essentials of matter and treatment it is a book of to-day. Its critical spirit and its impartial method are meant for a humanity which has outgrown the stage of fairy tales, realistic, romantic or even epic.

For the fairy tale, be it not ungratefully said, has walked the earth in many unchallenged disguises, and lingers amongst us to this day wearing, sometimes, amazingly heavy clothes. It lingers; and even it lingers with some assurance. Mankind has come of age, but the successive generations still demand artlessly to be amazed, moved and amused. Certain forms of innocent fun will never grow old, I suppose. But the secret of the long life of the fairy tale consists mainly in this, I suspect: that it is amusing to the writer thereof. Whatever public wants it supplies, it ministers first of all to his vanity in an intimate and delightful way. The pride of fanciful invention; the pride of that invention which soars (on goose's wings) into the empty blue is like the intoxication of an elixir sent by the gods above. And whether it is that the gods are unduly generous, or simply because the sight of human folly amuses their idle malice, that sort of felicity is easier attained pen in hand than the sober pride, always mingled with misgivings, of a single-minded observer and conscientious interpreter of reality. This is why the fairy tale, in its various disguises of optimism, pessimism, romanticism, naturalism and what not, will always be with us. And, indeed, that is very comprehensible; the seduction of irresponsible freedom is very great; and to be tied to the earth (even as the hewers of wood and drawers of water are tied to the earth) in the exercise of one's imagination, by every scruple of conscience and honour, may be considered a lot hard enough not to be lightly embraced. This is why novelists are comparatively rare. But we must not exaggerate

This world, even if one is tied fast to its earthy foundations by the subtle and tyrannical bonds of artistic conviction, is not such a bad place to write fiction in. At any rate, we can know of no other; an excellent reason for us to try to think as well as possible of the world we do know.

In this world, whose realities are discovered, interpreted, commented on, criticized and exposed in works of fiction, Mr. Galsworthy selects for the subject-matter of his book the Family, an institution which has been with us as long, I should think, as the oldest and the least venerable pattern of fairy tale. As Mr. Galsworthy, however, is no theorist but an observer, it is a definite kind of family that falls under his observation. It is the middle-class family; and even with more precision, as we are warned in the sub-title, an upper middle-class family anywhere at large in space and time, but a family, if not exactly of to-day, then of only last evening, so to say. Thus at the outset we are far removed from the vagueness of the traditional "once upon a time in a far country there was a king," which somehow always manages to peep through the solemn disguises of fairy tales masquerading as novels with and without purpose. The Forsytes walk the pavement of London and own some of London's houses. They wish to own more; they wish to own them all. And maybe they will. Time is on their side. The Forsytes never die— so Mr. Galsworthy tells us, while we watch them assembling in old Jolyon Forsyte's drawing room on the occasion of June Forsyte's engagement to Mr. Bosinney, incidentally an architect and an artist, but, by the only definition that matters, a man of no property whatever.

A family is not at first sight an alarming phenomenon. But Mr. Galsworthy looks at the Forsytes with the individual vision of a novelist seeking his inspiration amongst the realities of this earth. He points out to us this family's formidable character as a unit of society, as a reproduction in miniature of society itself. It is made formidable, he says, by the cohesion of its members (between whom there need not exist either affection or even sympathy) upon a concrete point, the possession of property.

The solidity of the foundation laid by Mr. Galsworthy for his fine piece of imaginative work becomes at once apparent. For whichever came first, family or property, in the beginnings of social organization, or whether they came together and were indeed at first scarcely distinguishable from each other, it is clear that in the close alliance of these two institutions society has found the way of its development and nurses the hope of its security. In their sense of property the Forsytes establish the consciousness of their right and the promise of their duration. It is an instinct, a primitive instinct. The practical faculty of the Forsytes has erected it into a principle; their idealism has expanded it into a sort of religion which has shaped their notions of happiness and decency, their prejudices, their piety, such thoughts as they happen to have and the very course of their passions. Life as a whole has come to be perceptible to them exclusively in terms of property. Preservation, acquisition—acquisition, preservation. Their laws, their morality, their art and their science appear to them, justifiably enough, consecrated to that double and unique end. It is the formula of their virtue.

In this world of Forsytes (who never die) organized in view of acquiring and preserving property, Mr. Galsworthy (who is no inventor of didactic fairy tales) places with the sure instinct of a novelist a man and a woman who are no Forsytes, it is true, but whom he presents as in no sense the declared adversaries of the great principle of property. They only happen to disregard it. And this is a crime. They are simply two people to whom life speaks imperatively in terms of love. And this is enough to establish their irreconcilable antagonism and to precipitate their unavoidable fate. Deprived naturally and suddenly of the support of laws and morality, of all human countenance, and even, in a manner of speaking, of the consolations of religion, they find themselves miserably crushed, both the woman and the man. And the principle of property is vindicated. The woman being the weaker, it is in her case vindicated with consummate cruelty. For a peculiar cowardice is one of the characteristics of this great and living principle. Strong in the worship of so many thousands and in the possession of so many millions, it starts with affright at the slightest challenge, it trembles before mere indifference, it directs its heaviest blows at the disinherited who should appear weakest in its sight. Irene's fate is made unspeakably atrocious, no less—but nothing more. Mr. Galsworthy's instinct and observation serve him well here. In Soames Forsyte's town house, whose front door stands wide open for half an hour or so on a certain foggy night, there is no room for tragedy. It is one of the temples of property, of a sort of unholy religion whose fundamental dogma, public ceremonies and awful secret rites, forming the subject matter of this remarkable novel, take no account of human dignity. Irene, as last seen crushed and alive within the hopeless portals, remains for us a poignantly pitiful figure and nothing more.

This then, roughly and summarily, is the book in its general suggestion. Going on to particulars which make up the intrinsic value of a work of art, it rests upon the subtle and interdependent relation of Mr. Galsworthy's intellect and feelings which form his temperament, and reveals Mr. Galsworthy's very considerable talent as a writer—a talent so considerable that it commands at once our respectful attention. The foundation of this talent, it seems to me, lies in a remarkable power of ironic insight combined with an extremely keen and faithful eye for all the phenomena on the surface of the life he observes. These are the purveyors of his imagination, whose servant is a style clear, direct, sane, illumined by a perfectly unaffected sincerity. It is the style of a man whose sympathy with mankind is too genuine to allow him the smallest gratification of his vanity at the cost of his fellow creatures. In its moderation it is a style sufficiently pointed to carry deep his remorseless irony and grave enough to be the dignified vehicle of his profound compassion. Its sustained harmony is never interrupted by those bursts of cymbals and fifes which some deaf people acclaim for brilliance. Before all, it is a style well under control, and therefore it never betrays this tender and ironic writer into an odious cynicism of laughter or tears. For there are two kinds of cynicism, the cynicism of the hyena and the cynicism of the crocodile, which last, by the way, commands all sorts of respects from the inhabitants of these Isles. Mr. Galsworthy remains always a man, whether he is amused or moved.

I am afraid that my unavowed intention in writing about this book (of which I have talked so much and said so little) has been discovered by now. Therefore I confess. Confession—public, I mean—is good for one's conscience. Such is my intention. And it would be easier to carry out if I only knew exactly the motives which prompt people to read novels. But I do not know them all. Some of us, I understand, take up a novel to gratify a natural malevolence, the author being supposed to hold the mirror up to the odiously ridiculous nature of our next-door neighbour. From laboriously collected information I am, however, led to believe that most people read novels for amusement. This is as it should be. But, whatever be their motives, I entertain towards all novel-readers (for reasons which must remain concealed from the readers of this paper) the feelings of warm and respectful affection. I would not try to deceive them for worlds. Never! This being understood, I go on to declare, in the peace of my heart and the serenity of my conscience, that if they want amusement they will find it between the covers of this book. They will find plenty of it in this episode in the history of the Forsytes, where the reconciliation of a father and son, the dramatic and poignant comedy of Soames Forsyte's marital relations, and the tragedy of Bosinney's failure are exposed to our gaze with the remorseless yet sympathetic irony of Mr. Galsworthy's art, in the light of the unquenchable fire burning on the altar of property. They will find amusement, and perhaps also something more lasting—if they care for it. I say this with all the reserves and qualifications which strict truth requires around every statement of opinion. Mr. Galsworthy may possibly be found disappointing by some, but he will never be found futile by any one, and never uninteresting by the most exacting. I myself, for instance, am not so sure of Bosinney's tragedy. But this hesitation of my mind, for which the author may not be wholly responsible after all, need only be mentioned and no more, in the face of his considerable achievement.

A GLANCE AT TWO BOOKS

THE national English novelist seldom regards his work—the exercise of his Art—as an achievement of active life by which he will produce certain definite effects upon the emotions of his readers, but simply as an instinctive, often unreasoned, outpouring of his own emotions. He does not go about building up his book with a precise intention and a steady mind. It never occurs to him that a book is a deed, that the writing of it is an enterprise as much as the conquest of a colony. He has no such clear conception of his craft. Writing from a full heart, he liberates his soul for the satisfaction of his own sentiment; and when he has finished the scene he is at liberty to strike his forehead and exclaim: "This is genius!"

Thackeray is reported to have done this, and there is no reason why any novelist of his type should not. He is, as a matter of fact, writing lyrically (a lyric is the expression of a mood); he is expressing his own moods: I take what the gods give me—he says in all humility, and when the godhead inspires him with what seems good to his heart, to his imagination, to his tenderness or to his indignation, he may say, and use the words literally, "This is genius!"

It is. And it is probably the reason why the distinctively English novelist is always at his best in denunciations of institutions, of types or of conventionalized society.

It is comparatively easy for us, when we are really moved by the clearness of our vision, to convince an audience that Messrs. A., B. and C. are callous, ferocious or cowardly. We should have to use much more conscious art to give a permanent impression of those gentlemen as purely altruist.

Thus Mr. Osborne, the hard merchant, father of Captain Osborne, is more definite and flawless than many of Thackeray's so-called good characters; and thus Mr. Pecksniff is, through scorn and dislike, rendered more memorable than the brothers Cheeryble. It is not perhaps so much that these distinguished writers were completely incapable of loving their fellow men simply as men, exposed to suffering, temptation and affliction, as that, neglecting the one indispensable thing, neglecting to use their powers of selection and observation, they emotionally excelled in rendering the disagreeable. And that is easy. To find beauty, grace, charm in the bitterness of truth is a graver task.

Thackeray, we imagine, did not love his gentle heroines. He did not love them. He was in love with the sentiments they represented. He was, in fact, in love with what does not exist—and that is why Amelia Osborne does not exist, either in colour, in shape, in grace, in goodness. Turgeniev probably did not love his Lisa, a most pathetic, pure, charming and profound creation, for what she was, in her creator's mind. He loved her disinterestedly, as it were, out of pure warmth of heart, as a human being in the tumult and hazard of life. And that is why we must feel, suffer and live with that wonderful creation. That is why she is as real to us as her stupid mother, as the men of the story, as the sombre Varvard, and all the others that may be called the unpleasant characters in "The House of Gentlefolk."

I have been reading two books in English which have attracted a good deal of intelligent attention, but neither seems to have been considered as attentively as they might have been from this point of view. The one, "The Island Pharisees," by Mr. John Galsworthy, is a very good example of the national novel: the other, "Green Mansions," by Mr. W. H. Hudson, is a proof that love, the pure love of rendering the external aspects of things, can exist side by side with the national novel in English letters.

Mr. Galsworthy's hero in "The Island Pharisees," during his pilgrimage right across the English social system, asks himself: "Why? Why is not the world better? Why are we all humbugs? Why is the social system so out of order?" And he gets no answer to his questions, for, indeed, in his mood no answer is possible, neither is an answer needed for the absolute value of the book. Shelton is dissatisfied with his own people, who are good people, with artists, whose "at homes" he drops into, with marriage settlements and wedding services, with cosmopolitan vagabonds, with Oxford dons, with policemen—with himself and his love.

The exposition of all the characters in the book is done with an almost unerring touch, with a touch indeed that recalls the sureness and the delicacy of Turgeniev's handling. They all live—and Mr. Galsworthy—or rather his hero, John Shelton, finds them all Pharisaic. It is as if he were championing against all these "good" people some intangible lost cause, some altruism, some higher truth that for ever seems to soar out of his grasp. It is not exactly that Shelton is made to uphold the bitter morality of the cosmopolitan vagabond; for Mr. Galsworthy is too good an artist and too good a philosopher to make his Louis Ferrand impossibly attractive or even possibly cynical.

Shelton upholds, not so much the fact as the ideal of honest revolt; he is the knight errant of a general idea.

Therein he ceases to resemble the other heroes of English fiction who are the champions of particular ideas, tilting sometimes at windmills (for the human power of self-deception is great), but with a particular foe always in their eye. Shelton distinctly does not couch his lance against a windmill. He is a knight errant, disarmed and faithful, riding forlorn to an inevitable defeat; his adversary is a giant of a thousand heads and a thousand arms, a monster at once perfectly human and altogether soulless. Though nobody dies in the book, it is really the record of a long and tragic adventure, whose tragedy is not so much in the event as in the very atmosphere, in the cold moral dusk in which the hero moves as if impelled by some fatal whisper, without a sword, corselet or helmet.

Amadis de Gaul would have struck a head off and counted it a doughty deed; Dickens would have flung himself upon pen and paper and made a caricature of the monster, would have flung at him an enormous joke vibrating with the stress of cheap emotions; Shelton, no legendary knight and being no humorist (but, like many simpler men, impelled by the destiny he carries within his breast), goes forth to be delivered, bound hand and foot, to the monster by his charming and limited Antonia. He is classed as an outsider by men in the best clubs, and his prospective mother-in-law tells him not to talk about things. He comes to grief socially, because in a world, which everyone is interested to go on calling the best of all possible worlds, he has insisted upon touching in challenge all the shields hung before all the comfortable tents: the immaculate shield of his fiancée, of his mother-in-law, of the best men in the best clubs. He gets himself called and thought of as Unsound; and there in his social world the monster has made an end of him.

This is the end of the book; and with it there comes into the world of letters the beginning of Mr. Galsworthy as a novelist. For, paradoxically, a society that could not stand a Hamlet in the flesh at any price will read about him and welcome him on the stage to the end of its own incorrigible existence. This book, where each page lives with an interest of its own, has for its only serious artistic defect that of not being long enough, and for its greatest quality that of a sincere feeling of compassionate regard for mankind expressed nationally through a fine indignation. Of the promise of its method, of the accomplished felicity of its phrasing, I have left myself no room to speak.

The innermost heart of "Green Mansions," which are the forests of Mr. Hudson's book, is tender, is tranquil, is steeped in that pure love of the external beauty of things that seems to breathe upon us from the pages of Turgeniev's work. The charming quietness of the style soothes the hard irritation of our daily life in the presence of a fine and sincere, of a deep and pellucid personality. If the other book's gift is lyric, "Green Mansions" comes to us with the tone of the elegy. There are the voices of the birds, the shadows of the forest leaves, the Indians gliding through them armed with their blowpipes, the monkeys peering sadly from above, the very spiders! The birds search for insects; spiders hunt their prey.

"Now as I sat looking down on the leaves and the small dancing shadow, scarcely thinking of what I was looking at, I noticed a small spider with a flat body and short legs creep cautiously out on to the upper surface of a small leaf. Its pale red colour, barred with velvet black, first drew my attention to it; for it was beautiful to the eye. . . ."

"It was beautiful to the eye," so it drew the attention of Mr. Hudson's hero. In that phrase dwells the very soul of the book whose voice is soothing like a soft voice speaking steadily amongst the vivid changes of a dream. Only you must note that the spider had come to hunt its prey, having mistaken the small dancing shadow for a fly, because it is there in the fundamental difference of vision lies the difference between book and book. The other type of novelist might say: "It attracted my attention because it was savage and cruel and beautiful only to the eye. And I have written of it here so that it may be hated and laughed at for ever. For of course being greedy and rapacious it was stupid also, mistaking a shadow for substance, like certain evil men, we have heard of, that go about crying up the excellence of the world."

PREFACE

To "The Shorter Tales of Joseph Conrad"

The idea of publishing a volume of selected stories has not been received without a good deal of hesitation on my part. So much in fact as to drive me into the dangerous attempt to disclose the state of the feelings with which I approach this explanatory preface. My hesitation was, I may say, of a private character; private in the sense of being rooted deep in my personality, and not easily explainable even to such good friends as it has been my fortune to find in the American public. The deep, complex (and at times even contradictory) feelings which make up the very essence of an author's attitude to his own creation are real enough, yet they may be, often are, but shapes of cherished illusions. Frail plants, you will admit, and fit only for the shade of solitary thought. Precious—perhaps? Yes. But by their very nature precious to only one man, to him in whose mind—or is it the heart?—they are rooted.

That consideration would seem to me conclusive against any one writing any preface whatever, if it were not for my ineradicable suspicion that in this world, which some philosophers have defined merely as a series of "vain appearances," our very illusions must have a practical meaning. Are they not as characteristic of an individual as his opinions, for instance, or the features of his face? In fact, being less controllable they must be even more dangerously revelatory. This

is an alarming consideration. But whether because of
a strain of native impudence, acquired callousness, or
inborn trust in the goodness of human nature, it has
not prevented me during the last few years from writing
a good many revelatory prefaces, for which I have not
been, so far, called to account. At any rate, no in-
censed man with a shotgun has yet called here to invite
me to desist. Thus encouraged, here I am again volunteering yet one more of these sincere confessions.

To begin with, I may venture to affirm that, however
spontaneous the initial impulse, not one of the stories
from which those included in this volume have been
selected was achieved without much conscious thought
bearing not only on the problems of their style but upon
their relation to life as I have known it, and on the
nature of my reactions to the particular instances as
well as to the general tenor of my personal experience.
This gave to each of the successive tales, composed at
various times and in varied mental conditions, a characteristic tone of its own. At least I thought so.
Later, when I had to consider my past work in detail,
in order to write the Author's Notes for my first collected edition, I was confirmed in my impression that
each of my short-story volumes had a consistent unity
of outlook covering the mingled subjects of civilization
and wilderness, of land life and life on the sea.

It would not be too much to say that this trait would
be apparent to the least critical of readers, in, for instance, the "Tales of Unrest." No story from that
volume is included in this collection for a reason which
will become apparent later to the patient reader of this
Preface. It is the very first collection of short stories
I ever published, with a range of scene including the
Malay Archipelago, rustic Brittany, Central Africa,
and the interior of an upper middle-class house in a

residential street of London. It also seems to me perfectly clear on the face of it, that the volume called "A Set of Six"—from which one story has been selected for this book—is very different in its consistent mood of clear and detached presentation from any other volume of short stories which I have published before or after. Yet, in Time, it covers almost the whole of the nineteenth century; and in Space it moves from South America through England and Russia to end in the south of Italy. A benevolent critic has remarked to me privately that it was the least atmospheric of all my works; and from my point of view I accepted this as a tribute to that inner consistency which I would claim for every set of my shorter tales. In the same way in the case of the volume "Within the Tides" I take the opinion expressed by one of the reviewers: "that the whole of the book seemed to produce the impression of being greater than its component parts" as a confirmation of my sentiment of having welded the diversities of subject and treatment into a consistency characteristic, in its nature, of a certain period of my literary production.

The friendly reader will understand how, holding that belief on the subject of my shorter productions, I would recoil at first from taking any of my stories out of their appointed places in the group to which they originally belonged. And this the more because their grouping was never the result of a preconceived plan. It "just happened." And things that "just happen" in one's work seem impressive and valuable because they spring from sources profounder than the logic of a deliberate theory suggested by acquiring learning, let us say, or by lessons drawn from analysed practice. And no one need quarrel for such a view with an artist for whom self-expression must, by definition, be the

principal object, if not the only *raison d'être*, of his existence. He will naturally take for his own, for better
or worse, all the characteristics of his work; since all
of them, intended or not intended, make up the individuality of his self-expression.

I suspect there are moments when what a man most
values in his work—I mean even a man of action—is
precisely the part the general mystery of things plays
in its shaping: the discovery of those qualities that have
"just happened" in that obscure region where honest
success or honourable failure is unconsciously elaborated. But there are moments too when one's idealism (for idealism is practical and sane and the enemy
of things that "just happen" and suchlike mysteries)
prompts one to take up a different, more precise view
of one's achievement—whatever it may be.

It must have been in one of those moments that
the suggestion of a selected volume of my shorter stories
came before me from my old friend and publisher,
Mr. F. N. Doubleday, who is an idealist and who
would simply hate to let anything "just happen" in
his business. His business, to my mind, consists,
mainly, in being the intermediary between certain men's
reveries and the wide-awake brain of the rest of the
world. Stated like this it seems a strangely fantastic
occupation; yet his ways of carrying it on are always of a
practical sort. I have learned to trust his conclusions
implicitly on that ground. Also, for reasons of a deeper
personal kind, having nothing to do with business, his
words have great weight with me. But in order to
reconcile my own idealism to the notion of taking the
stories out of their natural surroundings, out of their
native atmosphere as it were, some principle of selection had to be found. The only one that offered itself
with any chance of being acceptable was the principle of

classification by subject; one that, whatever its disadvantages, has at least the advantage of being immune from the infection of illusions.

But I soon found that for a writer whose simple purpose has ever been the sincere rendering of his own deeper and more sympathetic emotions in the face of his belief in men and things—the philosopher's "vain appearances" which yet have endured, poignant or amusing, for so many ages, moving processionally towards the End of the World, which when it comes will be the vainest thing of all—the principle was not so easy in its application as it seemed to be at first sight. Though I have been often classed as a writer of the sea I have always felt that I had no specialty in that or any other specific subject. It is true that I have found a full text of life on the sea, long before I thought of writing a line or even felt the faintest stirring towards self-expression by means of the printed word. Sea life had been my life. It had been my own self-sufficient, self-satisfying possession. When the change came over the spirit of my dream (Calderon said that "Life is a Dream") my past had, by the very force of my work, become one of the sources of what I may call, for want of a better word, my inspiration—of the inner force which sets the pen in motion. I would add here "for better or worse," if those words did not sound horribly ungrateful after so many proofs of sympathy from the public for which this particular Preface is destined.

As a matter of fact I have written of the sea very little if the pages were counted. It has been the scene, but very seldom the aim, of my endeavour. It is too late after all those years to try to keep back the truth; so I will confess here that when I launched my first paper boats in the days of my literary childhood, I aimed at an element as restless, as dangerous, as changeable as the sea, and even more vast;—the unappeasable ocean of human life. I trust this grandiloquent image will be accepted with an indulgent smile of the kind that is accorded to the lofty ambitions of well-meaning beginners. Much time has passed since, and I can assure my readers that I have never felt more humble than I do to-day while I sit tracing these words, and that I see now, more clearly than ever before, that indeed those were but paper boats, freighted with a grown-up child's dreams and launched innocently upon that terrible sea that, unlike the honest salt water of my early life, knows no hope of changing horizons but lies within the circle of an Eternal Shadow.

Approaching the problem of selection for this book in the full consciousness of my feelings, my concern was to give it some sort of unity, or in other words, its own character. Looking over the directive impulses of my writing life I discovered my guide in the one that had prompted me so often to deal with men whose existence was, so to speak, cast early upon the waters. Thus the characteristic trait of the stories included in this volume consists in the central figure of each being a seaman presented either in the relations of his professional life with his own kind, or in contact with landsmen and women, and embroiled in the affairs of that larger part of mankind which dwells on solid earth.

It would have been misleading to label those productions as sea tales. They deal with feelings of universal import, such, for instance, as the sustaining and inspiring sense of youth, or the support given by a stolid courage which confronts the unmeasurable force of an elemental fury simply as a thing that has got to be met and lived through with professional constancy. Of course, there is something more than mere ideas in those stories. I modestly hope that there are human beings in them, and also the articulate appeal of their humanity so strangely constructed from inertia and restlessness, from weakness and from strength and many other interesting contradictions which affect their conduct, and in a certain sense are meant to give a colouring to the actual events of the tale, and even to the response which is expected from the reader. To call them "studies of seamen" would have been pretentious and even misleading, in view of the obscurity of the individuals and the private character of the incidents. "Shorter Tales" is yet the best title I can think of for this collection. It commends itself to me by its non-committal character, which will neither raise false hopes nor awaken blind antagonisms.

Why a volume aiming at unity should be wilfully divided into two parts is explained by my desire to give prominence to the stories which begin them: "Youth," which is certainly a piece of autobiography ("emotions remembered in tranquillity"), and "Typhoon," which, defined from a purely descriptive point of view, is the shorter of the two storm-pieces which I have written at different times.

From another point of view, the "guiding" point of view (that is of each story being concerned with a man who is also a seaman), the first part deals with younger and the second with older men. I hardly need say that in the arrangement of those two parts there has been no attempt at chronological order.

Therefore let neither friend nor enemy look for the development of the writer's literary faculty in this collection. As far as that is concerned, the book is a jumble. The unity of purpose lies elsewhere. In Part First, "Youth" speaks for itself, both in its triumphant feeling and in its wistful regrets. The second story deals with what may be called the "*esprit de corps*," the deep fellowship of two young seamen meeting for the first time. Those two tales may be regarded as purely professional. Of the other two in Part First, one, it must be confessed, is written round a ship rather than round a seaman. The last, trying to render the effect of the fascination of a roving life, has the hard lot of a woman for its principal interest.

Part Two deals with men of a more mature age. There is no denying that in the typhoon which is being wrestled with by Captain McWhirr, it is the typhoon that takes on almost a symbolic figure. The next story is the story of a married seaman, badly married I admit, whose humanity to a pathetic waif spoils his life for him. The third is the story of a swindle, to be frank, planned on shore, but the sympathetic person is a seaman all right. The last may be looked upon as a story of a seaman's love for a very silent girl; but what I tried partly to suggest there was the existence of certain straightforward characters combining a natural ruthlessness with an unexpected depth of moral delicacy. Falk obeys the law of self-preservation pitilessly; but at the crucial moment of his bizarre love story he will not condescend to dodge the truth—the horrid truth! Finally, let me say that with the exception of "Youth" none of these stories is a record of experience in the absolute sense of the word. As I have said before in another preface, they are all authentic because they are the product of twenty years of life—my own life. Deliberate invention had little to do with their existence—if they do exist. In each there lurks more than one intention. The facts gleaned from hearsay or experience in the various parts of the globe were but opportunities offered to the writer. What he has done with them is matter for a verdict which must be left to the individual consciences of the readers.

COOKERY

A Preface to "A Handbook of Cookery for a Small House," by Jessie Conrad

Of all the books produced since the most remote ages by human talents and industry those only that treat of cooking are, from a moral point of view, above suspicion. The intention of every other piece of prose may be discussed and even mistrusted; but the purpose of a cookery book is one and unmistakable. Its object can conceivably be no other than to increase the happiness of mankind.

This general consideration, and also a feeling of affectionate interest with which I am accustomed to view all the actions of the writer, prompt me to set down these few words of introduction for her book. Without making myself responsible for her teaching (I own that I find it impossible to read through a cookery book), I come forward modestly but gratefully as a Living Example of her practice. That practice I dare pronounce most successful. It has been for many priceless years adding to the sum of my daily happiness.

Good cooking is a moral agent. By good cooking I mean the conscientious preparation of the simple food of everyday life, not the more or less skilful concoction of idle feasts and rare dishes. Conscientious cookery is an enemy to gluttony. The trained delicacy of the palate, like a cultivated delicacy of sentiment, stands in the way of unseemly excesses. The decency of our life is for a great part a matter of good taste, of the correct appreciation of what is fine in simplicity. The intimate influence of conscientious cooking by rendering easy the processes of digestion promotes the serenity of mind, the graciousness of thought, and that indulgent view of our neighbours' failings which is the only genuine form of optimism. Those are its titles to our reverence.

A great authority upon North American Indians accounted for the sombre and excessive ferocity characteristic of these savages by the theory that as a race they suffered from perpetual indigestion. The Noble Red Man was a mighty hunter but his wives had not mastered the art of conscientious cookery. And the consequences were deplorable. The Seven Nations around the Great Lakes and the Horse-tribes of the Plains were but one vast prey to raging dyspepsia. The Noble Red Men were great warriors, great orators, great masters of outdoor pursuits; but the domestic life of their wigwams was clouded by the morose irritability which follows the consumption of ill-cooked food. The gluttony of their indigestible feasts was a direct incentive to counsels of unreasonable violence. Victims of gloomy imaginings, they lived in abject submission to the wiles of a multitude of fraudulent medicine men—quacks—who haunted their existence with vain promises and false nostrums from the cradle to the grave.

It is to be remarked that the quack of modern civilization, the vendor of patent medicine, preys mainly upon the races of Anglo-Saxon stock who are also great warriors, great orators, mighty hunters, great masters of outdoor pursuits. No virtues will avail for happiness if the righteous art of cooking be neglected by the national conscience. We owe much to the fruitful meditations of our sages, but a sane view of life is, after all, elaborated mainly in the kitchen—the kitchen of the small house, the abode of the preponderant majority of the people. And a sane view of life excludes the belief in patent medicine. The conscientious cook is the natural enemy of the quack without a conscience; and thus his labours make for the honesty, and favour the amenity, of our existence. For a sane view of life can be no other than kindly and joyous, but a believer in patent medicine is steeped in the gloom of vague fears, the sombre attendants of disordered digestion.

Strong in this conviction, I introduce this little book to the inhabitants of the little houses who are the arbiters of the nation's destiny. Ignorant of the value of its methods, I have no doubt whatever as to its intention. It is highly moral. There cannot be the slightest question as to that; for is it not a cookery book? —the only product of the human mind altogether above suspicion.

In that respect no more need, or indeed can, be said. As regards the practical intention, I gather that no more than the clear and concise exposition of elementary principles has been the author's aim. And this too is laudable, because modesty is a becoming virtue in an artist. It remains for me only to express the hope that by correctness of practice and soundness of precept this little book will be able to add to the cheerfulness of nations.

THE FUTURE OF CONSTANTINOPLE

To the Editor of *The Times*, November 7, 1912.

Sir,

How long the last, Asiatic, phase of the history of the Turks—Sultanate of Damascus or Caliphate of Baghdad—may last, no one can say. That its European chapter is closed few only can doubt. But nobody will deny that a fierce scramble for Constantinople amongst the victors would be a most unseemly and disturbing complication.

The Serbs and Bulgars have no definite historical claim to advance. Greece has that, of course. But it must go very far back, to Byzantium—the old obscure colony. And really I cannot imagine this most democratic of kingdoms desiring a capital other than Athens —the very cradle of democracy, matchless in the wonders of its life and the vicissitudes of its history.

The Constantinople of which I think is not the Greek colony. It is the Imperial and symbolic city, one of the refuges of European civilization and the fit object of Europe's care. It should rest at last under the joint guarantee of all the Powers, after its infinitely varied, stormy, and tragic existence of august dominion, desperate wars, and abject slavery. It should find a dignified peace as an independent city, with a small territory, governed by an elected Senate (in which all the races of its population would be represented) and by—I won't call him its Burgomaster—let us say its

Patrician, as the executive head. The Balkan Powers might be co-jointly entrusted with his nomination. This would, to a certain extent, secure the share of Slavonic influence, since in the Senate the Greeks, I imagine, would predominate.

The independent Constantinople of my vision would be the splendid spiritual capital of the Balkan Peninsula naturally; its intellectual capital almost certainly. Commercially, too, as a free port, it would have all the chances, though Salonika may turn out a serious competitor. The various capitals of the Balkan States, residences of Courts and centres of political life, need not be jealous of the unique city which has done so much for the organization of mankind.

From its geographical position the Powers could easily give effective protection to that small municipal state. This plan, of course, implies free Dardanelles (but that seems already certain) and neutralized Bosphorus.

I am, Sir,

Your obedient servant,

J. Conrad.

November, 1912.

Perhaps you will allow me to expand a little the idea thrown out in my letter to *The Times*. Of its reception at large I know nothing—and perhaps it does not merit any sort of reception. Of course, when one puts down anything in the shape of a proposal one does think over the objections. I am not inclined to believe a notion right and feasible simply because it has occurred to me. I am not of that happy temperament. Still, when the first man who read my letter turned upon me with the words, "So you too, I see, have joined the ideologues," I believe my cheek blanched.

This was a pretty heavy charge to bring against a man conscious of being guilty of no worse crime than a little imagination. But it was not the severity of the indictment nor yet the knowledge that "ideologue" was the term of utmost scorn in the mouth of Napoleon I which disturbed me. I was not frightened or angry. I was extremely surprised. Ideologue! And I had meant my suggestion to be eminently practical. Practical—that is, strictly in accordance with the fitness of things.

For to any one with a little historical sense it is not in the fitness of things that Constantinople should become the capital of a Bulgarian kingdom. I do not wish to hurt youthful susceptibilities but frankly the city of the Bosphorus is too great, too illustrious for that fate. The crash of its fall reëchoed ominously from one end of Christendom to the other. Its liberation will send a mournful whisper of angry dismay through the Mussulman world. And the event at which we look is historically too momentous for anything but the indestructible city itself, the jewel of the Balkans and once the only luminous spot through nearly five centuries of European night, to be its commemorative monument.

If this be mere ideology then I am safe to say it has its inciting cause in a perfectly clear view of possible eventualities. Let us piously hope that the dawn of peace for the Peninsula will succeed this lurid conflagration. The waned Crescent is setting for ever; but to a calm observer the dawn seems a long way yet below the horizon. There will be many questions to be settled between themselves by the Balkan Children of the Cross—not to speak of some other outside Christians with views of their own. And what if amongst other things we were to see before many years a war between Greece and Bulgaria for the possession of Constantinople?

For in fact, historically and racially, Greece alone has a claim to Constantinople. But who is going to hand it over to her now? The Bulgarians are nearer, and, we are given to understand, intoxicated with their success.

But in this success they are not alone; and you cannot cut the crown of victory into four pieces and present each combatant with one fourth of immortal glory. The only sane way is to leave the Imperial City outside the field of dispute by a guaranteed agreement. There will be spoil enough—whether cut and dried already or likely to turn out an awkward morsel to carve—to repay the blood and treasure. For as to risks taken, there were none to be proud of in this enterprise.

As to the difficulty of staying the conquering army, that is only the lofty verbiage of elation. A disciplined army can always be stayed. The Russian army was stayed at San Stefano, and its victory, if not so swift and more dearly bought, was quite as complete. And indeed I would not deny to any of the combatants the satisfaction of triumphal entry. It is what comes after that will count.

Let us be sincere in this matter. This game was played for unequal stakes. For Turkey was staking her very head, while the Allies risked no more than a more or less severe blood-letting. We know that if the fortune of war had gone the other way, unanimous Europe would have stopped it with the *status quo* declaration and the hand of Turkey would have been stayed. This fact, of which not a single Balkanian of them all ever had the slightest doubt, should make them amenable to reason in the final settlement.

Nobody wishes to rob them of what is won. Constantinople would remain a joint possession, but with a life and dignity of its own, till—till another Eastern Empire comes into being. And I think it would be a rational arrangement. The same objector, while I was trying to parry the charge of being an ideologue, lunged at me with the affirmation that this was "working for Russia." I confess that I don't understand that thrust. I think that for some time the possession of Constantinople has ceased to be one of the immediate aims of Russian policy. But even so, I don't see how I am serving any such dark purpose. It would be certainly easier to make war on Bulgaria and take Constantinople from it than to lay violent hands on a defenceless free town under a European guarantee, to which Russia herself would be a party. Not to mention the fact that such an aggression would be considered a *casus belli* not only by one but by all the Balkan powers (including Greece), the joint guardians of the city under Europe's sanction.

But as far as Russia's desire of an open Black Sea is concerned, the plan should certainly meet with her approval. I don't think that Russia would like to see numerous batteries of Bulgarian guns on the heights behind the town, sealing up the Bosphorus most effectually even without the help of the Turks on the other side. Indeed, I don't believe Russia would contemplate such a possibility for a moment. And how would Bulgaria (or Greece for that matter) like the obligation of an unarmed capital and the limitations of her sovereign rights in the matter of defence?

A neutralized Bosphorus and a free Constantinople would arouse no envy, no jealousies, and give no offence. Constantinople, a religious and intellectual capital—a common possession, giving no umbrage to any one—a holy city of infinite prestige and incomparable beauty. And I am even thinking here of the Mohammedans. There will be, no doubt, many Muslims left in the peninsula, industrious and peaceable citizens of the Christian states. To them also Constantinople shall be a holy city; for the religious head of Mohammedans in Europe would be residing there, nominated by the Caliph in Asia, subject to confirmation by the Balkan powers.

It seems to me too that such a solution of the Constantinople problem would soothe to a certain extent the grief and unrest of Mussulmans all the world over. A consideration worth the notice of the European States which have become by conquest masters of Mohammedan territories.

The details of organization, in which all the races of the peninsula would be justly represented, cannot be a matter of insuperable difficulty. Every Bulgarian, Greek, Serb, or Montenegrin entering Constantinople should be able to say: "I am at home here. This ground on which I stand has been liberated by me and my brothers and this Imperial City, free to us all and subject to no one, is the splendid monument of our victory."

THE CONGO DIARY

INTRODUCTION

THE diary kept by Joseph Conrad in the Congo in 1890, or such of it as has survived (for there is no saying whether there was more or not), is contained in two small black penny notebooks, and is written in pencil. One carries his initials, J. C. K.—Joseph Conrad Korzeniowski. The first entry is dated June 13, 1890, but in the second notebook dates are practically discarded, and it is impossible to say when the last entry was made. And names of places, also, are practically discarded in the second notebook, while abounding in the first, so that, though we can see that the diary was begun at Matadi, we cannot discover where it was ended. The last place mentioned is Lulanga, far up the great sweep of the Congo River to the north of the Equator, but there remain some twenty-four pages of the diary beyond that entry in which no name whatsoever appears. It must, indeed, have been continued into the very heart of that immense darkness where the crisis of his story, "Heart of Darkness," is unfolded. We know from "A Personal Record" that he reached ultimately somewhere to the neighbourhood of Stanley Falls; and Stanley Falls are farther from Lulanga than Lulanga is from Stanley Pool.

And it is in this same book that we can read how the Polish boy, when nine years of age, looking upon a map of Africa, had put his finger upon its unexplored centre, and had said to himself, "When I grow up I shall go *there.*" Go there he did, and these notebooks are the first expression of his fulfilled resolve.

The map will enable the reader to plot out, with reasonable accuracy, the exact route followed by Conrad on his overland journey, from Matadi, which is about one hundred miles above the mouth of the Congo, to Nselemba, on or near the southeast corner of Stanley Pool—a distance of probably more than two hundred and fifty miles from Matadi—where it was that he joined the *Roi des Belges*, as second in command, for the up-river voyage. The places and streams alluded to on this overland journey have been given on the map in Conrad's own spelling, even where their names have been altered (unless beyond recognition, which may have happened in certain instances) in existing atlases, many of which have been examined, or can only be placed approximately, owing to their not being mentioned at all. The mapping of the Congo is not in a very advanced state, and, what with the paucity of the entries and the contradictory nature of the information, precise accuracy is not attainable. All the same, it is easy enough to trace the general line of his march, which lay much nearer the banks of the Congo than lies the railway which now runs between Matadi and Kinshasa on Stanley Pool.

The following is a reproduction of the first notebook alone—not, however, of the list of names, persons, books, stores, and the calculations that fill the last pages—consisting of thirty-two manuscript pages, not all of which are full, and twelve of which are further curtailed by Conrad's sectional drawings of the day's march. The given spelling and abbreviations have been adhered to throughout—they help to heighten its true flavour—but the paragraphing and the punctuation have been freely altered.

I may mention that these two notebooks are now preserved in the library of Harvard University, and

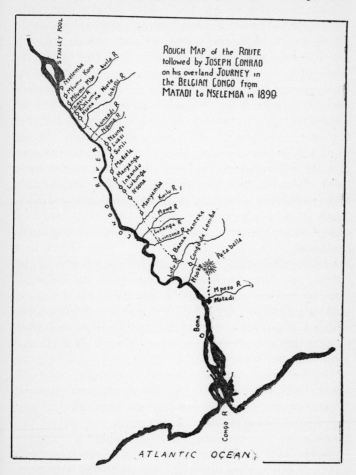

ROUGH MAP of the ROUTE
followed by JOSEPH CONRAD
on his overland JOURNEY in
the BELGIAN CONGO from
MATADI to NSELEMBA in 1890

that when I was in America in 1925 I saw them again in their new and permanent home and checked the text once more.

As to the appended footnotes, their chief purpose has been to show how closely some of the earlier pages of "Heart of Darkness" are a recollection of Conrad's own Congo journey. This story was serialized in *Blackwood's Magazine* between February and April, 1899, and I remember Conrad telling me that its 40,000 words occupied only about a month in writing. When we consider the painful, slow labour with which he usually composed, we can perceive how intensely vivid his memories of this experience must have been, and, to judge from the parallel passages, how intensely actual. But then the notebook only goes to prove the almost self-evident contention that much of Conrad's work is founded upon autobiographical remembrance. Conrad himself wrote of this story in his Author's Note to the new edition of the "Youth" volume in which it appeared: "'Heart of Darkness' is quite as authentic in fundamentals as 'Youth' . . . it is experience pushed a little (and only a little) beyond the actual facts of the case." If only he had kept a diary of his meeting and association with Kurtz!

The pages of The Concord Edition of "Youth" —the edition always referred to in the notes—which bear direct reference to the first volume of the diary, are only three, 70–72, but in these few pages there are an astonishing number of touches strongly reminiscent of the diary. One would argue, indeed, that he must have consulted the diary when writing the story, but Mrs. Conrad assures me that it was not so. Twice had she saved it from the wastepaper basket, and probably by the time "Heart of Darkness" came to be written Conrad had forgotten all about it, or did not dream that it had survived. He never spoke to me of it, and I never heard of its existence until after his death.

The second notebook, which is an entirely technical

account of Congo navigation, written, no doubt, in relation to the then river charts, is not printed here, simply because it has no personal or literary interest. It is much longer than the first notebook, and is contained on seventy-nine pages, apart from several pages of rough outline maps. I reproduce a portion of one page, in order to show a sample:

"11. N. (A) Long reach to a curved point. Great quantity of dangerous snags along the star^d shore. Follow the slight bend of the shore with caution. The Middle of the Channel is a S—B— [sand bank] always covered. The more northerly of the two islands has its lower end bare of trees covered with grass and light green low bushes, then a low flat, and the upper end is timbered with light trees of a darker green tint."

It will be seen from this passage, which, though typical, is less technical than most, that the second notebook is not really, like the first, so much in the nature of a diary as of a specific aid to navigation. But those who recall the river journey in "Heart of Darkness," with its dangers and its difficulties, will perceive how this notebook, too, has played its special and impersonal part in the construction of that story.

The title-page of the first notebook is almost all torn out, but the title-page of the second reads, "Up-river Book, commenced 3 August 1890, S.S. *Roi des Belges*." Long ago, when I was making, from Conrad's dictation, a list of the ships he had sailed in, he wrote opposite *Roi des Belges*—"'Heart of Darkness,' 'Out-post.'" And, in truth, hints for "Heart of Darkness," reminders of "Heart of Darkness," lie thick upon the pages of the first notebook, though "An Outpost of Progress"—"the lightest part of the loot I carried off from Central

Africa," to quote his Author's Note to "Tales of Unrest," in which it was published—is only visible in the diary by the implication of the tropical African atmosphere.

No other diary of Conrad's is extant, and I am very sceptical as to whether he ever kept another. He was not at all that type of man, and his piercing memory for essentials was quite sufficient for him to recreate powerfully vanished scenes and figures for the purposes of his work. In 1890, of course, he had published nothing, and though we know that the unfinished MS. (seven chapters) of "Almayer's Folly" accompanied him on his Congo journey—"A Personal Record" describes how it was nearly lost on the river—yet it is doubtful whether he seriously envisaged its appearance in print at a future date. It was largely the breakdown of Conrad's health, due to this very trip, that caused him finally to abandon the sea, and if he had not abandoned the sea, how could he have become a novelist in the accepted sense? Unless we assume that genius must always find means of full expression—a big assumption and quite beyond proof—we owe it really to an accident that Conrad adopted writing as a career. Without this journey, and, therefore, without this diary, where would have been the great Conrad novels?

Thirty-four years to a day from beginning the second notebook, Conrad died—August 3, 1924. Reading it again, I find, as I am continually finding, how many things there are which I would have liked to ask him and never did ask him, and how much I want to know, which I never now can know. Well, that is always what happens when our friends depart. This diary is only a strange, tantalizing fragment and must eternally remain so. Yet it has a value of its own, both real and romantic, and I am glad to be able to give it to the world.

RICHARD CURLE.

THE DIARY

Arrived at Matadi[1] on the 13th of June, 1890.

Mr. Gosse, chief of the station (O. K.) retaining us for some reason of his own.

Made the acquaintance of Mr. Roger Casement,[2] which I should consider as a great pleasure under any circumstances and now it becomes a positive piece of luck. Thinks, speaks well, most intelligent and very sympathetic.

Feel considerably in doubt about the future. Think just now that my life amongst the people (white) around here cannot be very comfortable. Intend avoid acquaintances as much as possible.

Through Mr. R. C. have made the acquain^{ce} of Mr. Underwood, the Manager of the English Factory (Hatton & Cookson) in Kalla Kalla. Av^{ge} com^{al}— hearty and kind. Lunched there on the 21st.

24th. Gosse and R. C. gone with a large lot of ivory down to Boma. On G.['s] return intend to start up the river. Have been myself busy packing ivory in casks. Idiotic employment. Health good up to now.

Wrote to Simpson, to Gov. B., to Purd.,[3] to Hope,[4]

---

[1]On his voyage from Europe presumably.

[2]Afterwards the notorious Sir Roger Casement, who was hanged for treason on August 3, 1916—the very date on which Conrad died eight years later. At this period Casement was in the employ of a commercial firm in the Congo. In 1898 he became British Consul in the Congo Free State.

[3]Probably Captain Purdy, an acquaintance of Conrad.

[4]Conrad's old friend, now living in Essex, Mr. G. F. W. Hope. In 1900 Conrad dedicated "Lord Jim" to Mr. and Mrs. Hope, "with grateful affection after many years of friendship."

to Capt. Froud,[1] and to Mar.[2]. Prominent characteristic of the social life here; people speaking ill of each
other.[3]

Saturday, 28th June. Left Matadi with Mr. Harou[4]
and a caravan of 31 men.[5] Parted with Casement in a
very friendly manner. Mr. Gosse saw us off as far as the
State station.

First halt, M'poso. 2 Danes in Company.[6]

Sund[ay], 29th. Ascent of Pataballa sufficiently fa-
tiguing. Camped at 11 A.M. at Nsoke river. Mosquitos
[always spelt thus].

Monday, 30th. To Congo da Lemba after passing
black rocks. Long ascent. Harou giving up.[7] Bother.
Camp bad. Water far. Dirty. At night Harou
better.

Tuesday, 1st July. Left early in a heavy mist,
marching towards Lufu river. Part route through
forest on the sharp slope of a high mountain. Very
long descent. Then market place from where short

---

[1]The then Secretary of the London Ship-Master's Society. See "A Personal Record" (Concord Edition), p. 7. "Dear Captain Froud—it is impossible not to pay him the tribute of affectionate familiarity at this distance of years—had very sound views as to the advancement of knowledge
and status for the whole body of the officers of the mercantile marine."

[2]Probably Marguerite Poradowska, his aunt.

[3]This was also a failing of the white men at the "Central Station" in
"Heart of Darkness."

[4]Harou was an official of the Etat Indépendant du Congo Belge.

[5]Compare "Heart of Darkness," p. 70: "Next day I left that station at
last with a caravan of 60 men for a 200-mile tramp." On 13 out of the 19
travelling days taken by Conrad on this overland journey he kept a record
of the distance covered, and it totals 197½ miles.

[6]Curiously enough, the identity of these two Danes was discovered by
Monsieur G. Jean-Aubry in Brussels early in 1925. Not knowing that they
were mentioned in the diary, he omitted to take names or particulars.

[7]He seems to have been constantly unwell and one may compare "Heart
of Darkness," p. 71: "I had a white companion too, not a bad chap,
but rather too fleshy, and with the exasperating habit of fainting on the hot
hillsides, miles away from the least bit of shade or water."

walk to the bridge (good) and camp. V. G. Bath.
Clear river. Feel well. Harou all right. 1st chicken,
2 p. [m.] No sunshine to-day.

Wednesday, 2nd July. Started at 5:30 after a sleepless night. Country more open. Gently undulating
hills. Road good, in perfect order. (District of Lu-
kungu.) Great market at 9:30. Bought eggs and
chickens. Feel not well to-day. Heavy cold in the
head. Arrived at 11 at Banza Manteka. Camped on
the market place. Not well enough to call on the
missionary. Water scarce and bad. Camp^g place
dirty. 2 Danes still in Company.

Thursday, 3rd July. Left at 6 a. m. after a good
night's rest. Crossed a low range of hills and entered a
broad valley, or rather plain, with a break in the middle.
Met an off^er of the State inspecting. A few minutes
afterwards saw at a camp^g place the dead body of a
Backongo. Shot?[1] Horrid smell.

Crossed a range of mountains, running N. W.—S. E.
by a low pass. Another broad flat valley with a deep
ravine through the centre. Clay and gravel. Another
range parallel to the first mentioned, with a chain of low
foothills running close to it. Between the two came to
camp on the banks of the Luinzono river. Camp^g
place clean. River clear. Gov^t Zanzibari[2] with register. Canoe. 2 Danes camp^g on the other bank.
Health good.

General tone of landscape gray-yellowish (dry grass)

---

[1]Compare "Heart of Darkness," p. 71: "Once a white man in an unbut-
toned uniform camping on the path . . . was looking after the upkeep
of the road, he declared. Can't say I saw any road or any upkeep, unless
the body of a middle-aged negro with a bullet-hole in the forehead, upon
which I absolutely stumbled three miles further on, may be considered as
a permanent improvement."

[2]Compare "Heart of Darkness," p. 71, in which he mentioned his meeting
with a white man, who was accompanied by "an armed escort of lank
Zanzibaris."

with reddish patches (soil) and clumps of dark green vegetation scattered sparsely about. Mostly in steep gorges between the high mountains or in ravines cutting the plain.[1]

Noticed Palma Christi—Oil Palm. Very straight, tall and thick trees in some places. Name not known to me. Villages quite invisible. Infer their existence from calbashes [sic] suspended to palm trees for the "Malafu." Good many caravans and travellers. No women, unless on the market place.

Bird notes charming. One especially a flute-like note. Another, kind of "boom" ressembling [sic] the very distant baying of a hound. Saw only pigeons and a few green parroquets. Very small and not many. No birds of prey seen by me.[2]

Up to 9 A. M. sky clouded and calm. Afterwards gentle breeze from the Nth generally and sky clearing. Nights damp and cool. White mists on the hills up about half way. Water effects very beautiful this morning. Mists generally raising before sky clears.

Distance 15 miles. General direction N. N. E.— S. S. W.

Friday, 4th July. Left camp at 6 A. M. after a very unpleasant night. Marching across a chain of hills and then in a maze of hills. At 8:15 opened out into an undulating plain. Took bearings of a break in the chain of mountains on the other side. Bearing N. N. E. Road passes through that. Sharp ascents up very steep hills not very high. The higher mountains recede sharply and show a low hilly country. At 9:30 market

---

[1] In "Heart of Darkness," p. 70, the country of the march is described as "a stamped-in network of paths spreading over the empty land, through long grass, through burnt grass, through thickets, down and up hilly ravines, up and down stony hills ablaze with heat."

[2] These natural history observations are curious, as Conrad practically never showed the slightest interest in such subjects.

place. At 10 passed R. Lukanga and at 10:30 camped on the Mpwe R.

To-day's march. Direction N. N. E.½.—N. Dist^{ce} 13 miles.

Saw another dead body lying by the path in an attitude of meditative repose.[1]

In the evening three women, of whom one albino, passed our camp; horrid chalky white with pink blotches; red eyes; red hair; features very negroid and ugly. Mosquitos. At night when the moon rose heard shouts and drumming in distant villages.[2] Passed a bad night.

Saturday, 5th July. Left at 6:15. Morning cool, even cold, and very damp. Sky densely overcast. Gentle breeze from N. E. Road through a narrow plain up to R. Kwilu. Swift flowing and deep, 50 yds. wide. Passed in canoes. After^{ds} up and down very steep hills intersected by deep ravines. Main chain of heights running mostly N. W.—S. E. or W. and E. at times. Stopped at Manyamba. Camp^g place bad—in a hollow—water very indifferent. Tent set at 10:15. N. N. E. Dist^{ce} 12 m.

To-day fell into a muddy puddle—beastly! The fault of the man that carried me. After camp^g went to a small stream, bathed and washed clothes. Getting jolly well sick of this fun.

To-morrow expect a long march to get to Nsona, 2 days from Manyanga. No sunshine to-day.

Sunday, 6th July. Started at 5:40. The route at first hilly, then, after a sharp descent, traversing a

---

[1]The most "Conradesque" phrase in the diary.

[2]Compare "Heart of Darkness," p. 71: "Perhaps on some quiet night the tremor of far-off drums, sinking, swelling, a tremor vast, faint; a sound weird, appealing, suggestive, and wild—and perhaps with as profound a meaning as the sound of bells in a Christian country."

broad plain. At the end of it a large market place. At 10 sun came out. After leaving the market passed another plain, then, walking on the crest of a chain of hills, passed 2 villages and at 11 arrived at Nsona. Village invisible.

Direction about N. N. E. Distance 18 miles.

In this camp (Nsona) there is a good camp^g place. Shady, water far and not very good. This night no mosquitos owing to large fires, lit all round our tent. Afternoon very close: night clear and starry.

Monday, 7th July. Left at 6, after a good night's rest, on the road to Inkandu, which is some distance past Lukunga Govt. station. Route very accidented.[1] Succession of round steep hills. At times walking along the crest of a chain of hills. Just before Lukunga our carriers took a wide sweep to the southward till the station bore Nth. Walking through long grass for $1\frac{1}{2}$ hours. Crossed a broad river about 100 feet wide and 4 deep.

After another $\frac{1}{2}$ hour's walk through manioc plantations in good order rejoined our route to the E^d of the Lukunga sta^{on}, walking along an undulating plain towards the Inkandu market on a hill. Hot, thirsty and tired. At 11 arrived on the m^{ket} place. About 200 people. Business brisk. No water; no camp^g place. After remaining for one hour left in search of a resting place. Row with carriers. No water. At last about $1\frac{1}{2}$ P. M. camped on an exposed hill side near a muddy creek. No shade. Tent on a slope. Sun heavy. Wretched.

Direction N. E. by N.—Distance 22 miles.

Night miserably cold. No sleep. Mosquitos.

Tuesday, 8th July. Left at 6 A. M. About ten

---

[1] An odd Gallicism. Conrad knew French long before he knew English; moreover, he was naturally talking much French at this time.

minutes from camp left main Gov^t path for the Manyanga track. Sky overcast. Rode up and down
all the time, passing a couple of villages. The country
presents a confused wilderness of hills, landslips on their
sides showing red. Fine effect of red hill covered in
places by dark green vegetation. ½ hour before beginning the descent got a glimpse of the Congo. Sky
clouded.

To-day's march—3 h. General direction N. by E.
Dist^{ce} 9½ miles.

Arrived at Manyanga at 9 A. M. Received most
kindly by Messrs. Heyn and Jaeger. Most comfortable
and pleasant halt.

Stayed here till the 25. Both have been sick. Most
kindly care taken of us. Leave with sincere regrets.

Friday, the 25th July, 1890. Left Manyanga at 2½
P. M. with plenty of hammock carriers. H. lame
and not in very good form. Myself ditto but not lame.
Walked as far as Mafiela and camped—2 h.

Saturday, 26th. Left very early. Road ascending
all the time. Passed villages. Country seems thickly
inhabited. At 11 arrived at large market place. Left
at noon and camped at 1 P. M.

General direction E ½ N-W ½ S. Sun visible at 8 A. M.
Very hot. Distance 18 miles.

Sunday, 27th. Left at 8 A. M. Sent luggage carriers
straight on to Luasi, and went ourselves round by the
Mission of Sutili. Hospitable reception by Mrs.
Comber. All the missio. absent. The looks of the
whole establishment eminently civilized and very
refreshing to see after the lots of tumbled down hovels
in which the State & Company agents are content to
live. Fine buildings. Position on a hill. Rather
breezy.

Left at 3 P. M. At the first heavy ascent met Mr.

Davis, Miss., returning from a preaching trip. Rev. Bentley away in the south with his wife. This being off the road, no section given.[1]

Distance traversed about 15 miles. Gen. direction E. N. E.

At Luasi we get on again on to the Gov^t road.

Camped at 4½ P. M. with Mr. Heche in company. To-day no sunshine. Wind remarkably cold. Gloomy day.

Monday, 28th. Left camp at 6:30 after breakfasting with Heche. Road at first hilly. Then walking along the ridges of hill chains with valleys on both sides. The country more open and there is much more trees[2] growing in large clumps in the ravines.

Passed Nzungi and camped, 11, on the right bank of the Ngoma, a rapid little river with rocky bed. Village on a hill to the right.

General direction E. N. E.—Distance 14 miles.

No sunshine. Gloomy cold day. Squalls.

Tuesday, 29th. Left camp at 7, after a good night's rest. Continuous ascent; rather easy at first. Crossed wooded ravines and the river Lunzadi by a very decent bridge. At 9 met Mr. Louette escorting a sick agent of the comp^y back to Matadi. Looking very well. Bad news from up the river. All the steamers disabled—one wrecked.[3] Country wooded. At 10:30 camped at Inkissi.

---

[1]Sections of the day's marches, with numerous names on them, were given under the following dates: July 3rd, 4th, 5th, 6th, 7th, 8th, 25th, 28th, 29th, 30th, 31st, August 1st.

[2]One of the few un-English phrases in the diary. By 1890 Conrad had been a British subject for six years, but he never learnt the language until he was grown up.

[3]Compare "Heart of Darkness," p. 72: "One of them [the white men at the Central Station] . . . informed me with great volubility and many digressions . . . that my steamer was at the bottom of the river."

General direction E. N. E.—Dist^{ce} 15 miles.

Sun visible at 6:30. Very warm day.

Inkissi River very rapid; is about 100 yards broad. Passage in canoes. Banks wooded very densely, and valley of the river rather deep, but very narrow.

To-day did not set the tent, but put up in Gov^t shimbek. Zanzibari[1] in charge—very obliging. Met ripe pineapple for the first time. On the road to-day passed a skeleton tied up to a post. Also white man's grave—no name—heap of stones in the form of a cross. Health good now.

Wednesday, 30th. Left at 6 A. M. intending to camp at Kinfumu. Two hours sharp walk brought me to Nsona na Nsefe. Market. ½ hour after Harou arrived very ill with billious [*sic*] attack and fever. Laid him down in Gov^t shimbek.

Dose of ipec^a. Vomiting bile in enormous quantities. At 11 gave him 1 gramme of quinine and lots of hot tea. Hot fit ending in heavy perspiration. At 2 P. M. put him in hammock and started for Kinfumu. Row with carriers all the way.[2] Harou suffering much through the jerks of the hammock. Camped at a small stream. At 4 Harou better; fever gone.

General direction N. E. by E. ½ E. Distance 13 miles.

Up till noon sky clouded and strong N. W. wind very chilling. From 1 P. M. to 4 P. M. sky clear and a very hot day. Expect lots of bother with carriers to-morrow. Had them all called and made a speech,

---

[1]See note, p. 163.

[2]Compare "Heart of Darkness," p. 71: "Then he [the white man with him] got fever, and had to be carried in a hammock slung under a pole. As he weighed sixteen stone I had no end of rows with the carriers."

which they did not understand.[1] They promise good behaviour.

Thursday, 31st. Left at 6. Sent Harou ahead, and followed in ½ an hour.[2]

Road presents several sharp ascents, and a few others easier but rather long. Notice in places sandy surface soil instead of hard clay as heretofore; think however that the layer of sand is not very thick and that the clay would be found under it. Great difficulty in carrying Harou. Too heavy—bother![3] Made two long halts to rest the carriers. Country wooded in valleys and on many of the ridges.

At 2:30 P. M. reached Luila at last, and camped on right bank. Breeze from S. W.

General direction of march about N. E. ½ E. Distance, est^d 16 miles.

Congo very narrow and rapid. Kinzilu rushing in. A short distance up from the mouth, fine waterfall. Sun rose red. From 9 A. M. infernally hot day. Harou very little better. Self rather seedy. Bathed. Luila about 60 feet wide. Shallow.

Friday, 1st of August, 1890. Left at 6:30 A. M. after a very indifferently passed night. Cold, heavy mists. Road in long ascents and sharp dips all the way to Mfumu Mbé. After leaving there, a long and painful climb up a very steep hill; then a long descent to Mfumu Kono, where a long halt was made. Left at 12:30 P. M. towards Nselemba. Many ascents. The aspect of the country entirely changed. Wooded hills

---

[1] Compare "Heart of Darkness," p. 71: ". . . one evening, I made a speech in English with gestures, not one of which was lost to the sixty pairs of eyes before me."

[2] Compare "Heart of Darkness," pp. 71–2: ". . . the next morning I started the hammock off in front all right."

[3] Compare "Heart of Darkness," p. 71: ". . . he [the white man with him] weighed sixteen stone. . . ."

with openings. Path almost all the afternoon thro' a forest of light trees with dense undergrowth.

After a halt on a wooded hillside, reached Nselemba at 4:10 P. M. Put up at Gov^t shanty. Row between the carriers and a man, stating himself in Gov^t employ, about a mat. Blows with sticks raining hard. Stopped it.

Chief came with a youth about 13 suffering from gun-shot wound in the head. Bullet entered about an inch above the right eyebrow, and came out a little inside the roots of the hair, fairly in the middle of the brow in a line with the bridge of the nose. Bone not damaged apparently. Gave him a little glycerine to put on the wound made by the bullet on coming out.

Harou not very well. Mosquitos—frogs—beastly! Glad to see the end of this stupid tramp. Feel rather seedy. Sun rose red. Very hot day. Wind S^th.

General direction of march N. E. by N. Distance about 17 miles.[1]

[1] The journey from Matadi to this point by Stanley Pool took nineteen travelling days. Compare "Heart of Darkness," p. 72: "On the fifteenth day I came in sight of the big river [Congo] again and hobbled into the Central Station."

THE END